WYCLIFFE COLLEGE

T0326714

Arnold Edinborough is President and Chief Executive Officer of the Council for Business and the Arts in Canada and the author of *Some Camel ... Some Needle and Other Thoughts for the Day*. He is well known as a columnist, editor, and speaker.

Since Wycliffe College was founded 100 years ago as an Anglican theological college in Toronto, it has had six principals. To celebrate the influence they and the college have had on the religious life of Canada and other countries, six writers have collaborated to produce *The Enduring Word*.

The lives of the five past principals have been written by Jacob Jocz, T.R. Millman, R.K. Harrison, Alan Hayes, and Robert Finch. Arnold Edinborough's profile of the present principal, Dr Reginald Stackhouse, provides insight into both the man and the kinds of cha lenges he faces as he leads Wycliffe into its second century.

Rich in anecdote and sound in research, *The Enduring Word* is a centennial volume whose interest goes far beyond the college and its members past and present.

100

1877·1977

The Enduring Word

A Centennial History of
Wycliffe College

Edited by Arnold Edinborough

PUBLISHED FOR WYCLIFFE COLLEGE BY

UNIVERSITY OF TORONTO PRESS

TORONTO   BUFFALO   LONDON

©University of Toronto Press 1978
Toronto   Buffalo   London
Reprinted 2017
ISBN 978-0-8020-3356-7 (cloth)
ISBN 978-1-4875-9829-7 (paper)

Canadian Cataloguing in Publication Data

Main entry under title:
The Enduring word
ISBN 978-0-8020-3356-7 (bound).   ISBN 978-1-4875-9829-7 (pbk.)
1. Wycliffe College — History. I. Edinborough,
Arnold, 1922 —
BV4160.W96E54 .   207'.713'541   C78-001246-1

Contents

Foreword
vii

Beginnings:
The Principalship of James Paterson Sheraton
JAKOB JOCZ
3

Expansion:
The Principalship of T.R. O'Meara
THOMAS R. MILLMAN
23

Depression:
The Principalship of R.B. McElheran
ALAN HAYES
40

War and Peace:
The Principalship of Ramsay Armitage
ROBERT FINCH
65

The Turbulent Years:
The Principalship of Leslie Hunt
ROLAND HARRISON
88

Into the Second Century:
The Principalship of Reginald Stackhouse
ARNOLD EDINBOROUGH
107

Index
127

Foreword

When Wycliffe College was half a century old in 1927, a jubilee volume telling of its founding and of the first fifty highly successful years was undertaken by the college. It was a story of triumph born out of controversy; a story also of remarkable missionary achievement for a small colonial college which had grown in that time to be the largest single theological college in the Anglican communion.

Wycliffe this year celebrates its hundredth anniversary. The second fifty years have been lived through a very different climate. First came the Great Depression when the college faced stringent cut-backs as a result of the deterioration of its investments in land. During that time, too, there was a strong socialist movement within universities — a movement that did not find a happy home at Wycliffe.

The depression was followed by World War II, during which the college was stripped for a second time in twenty-five years of some of its professors and many of its potential students.

By 1946, however, the college was once more ready to expand and to take care of the increasing number of parishes being created by Canada's post-war population boom. While seeking to satisfy the demands of the local scene, Wycliffe was, as always, conscious of the missionary field and the priests necessary for the far west and north of this vast land. By the 1960s, as the country approached its one hundredth birthday and the college its ninetieth, another depression had set in — not economic but spiritual and philosophical. It was fashionable to assume that God was dead and there were books written on the solemn, nevertheless silly, assumption that there was a 'Christian atheism.' In Canada, what had been started by people like

Bishop John Robinson in England and Thomas Altizer in the United States, was fueled by such books as *The Comfortable Pew* by Pierre Berton (commissioned by the Anglican Church of Canada) and *Let God Go Free* by the Reverend Ernest Harrison.

All this now seems to be behind us. Yet, as the college celebrates its centennial year of service to the Christian community, there are still uncertainties of direction and, alas, uncertainties of faith. Not, of course, in the college. Wycliffe looks still to the kind of future it can face because of its kind of past. It has been resilient, strong in its lay affiliation, and constantly anchored on the study of the New Testament and the proclamation of its message.

Whereas the fiftieth anniversary volume dealt with the history of the first fifty years in a conventional fashion (and is still good reading for those who have yet to make its acquaintance), this centennial book is different in concept.

The Christian message, as bodied forth in both the lives and doctrines of Wycliffe faculty and graduates over the years, has been concerned with the person and the relationship of a person with his God. It follows that the college itself must have owed a great deal to the persons who have assumed its direction as principal. The scheme, therefore, of this book is simple: the history of the past one hundred years is seen through the achievement of the six principals who have directed its fortunes through that century. They have been men of greatly varying capacities and of a variety of talents. Some have been scholars, some have been administrators, all have been evangelists.

To proclaim their variety, I have asked four members of the present college faculty to write about a particular principal. The fifth author, Professor Robert Finch, though not a student at Wycliffe, lived in the college as a member of the faculty of the University of Toronto for over fifteen years. In that time he not only became identified with the college, but was a senior person to whom many a theological student could tell his troubles or to whom he could expound his ideas. That he is also a poet is clear from his luminous account of Dr Ramsay Armitage's years at the helm.

Dr Jakob Jocz, a theologian, was asked to contribute the first chapter because the whole genesis of Wycliffe was embedded in theological controversy and only after that controversy has been delineated is it possible to see the achievement of Principal Sheraton in its proper context.

Dr R.K. Harrison and Dr Thomas R. Millman are well known to generations of Wycliffe students and each has personal knowledge of the people about whom he writes.

Professor Alan Hayes, who tells of the McElheran years, is a younger member of faculty whose approach has, of necessity, been through the printed documents of the time. His contribution therefore has a somewhat different slant from that of the other writers.

I count it an honour to have been asked to edit the volume and to look, not back at the past, but to the future in projecting Wycliffe and Wycliffe principles into the next century, a task I should never have been able to undertake had it not been for the constant advice and information proferred by Dr Reg Stackhouse, the principal under whose guidance the college now makes its entry into that second century.

A. EDINBOROUGH
Toronto, 1 July 1977

THE ENDURING WORD:

A CENTENNIAL HISTORY OF WYCLIFFE COLLEGE

Beginnings

The Principalship of
James Paterson Sheraton
1877-1906

JAKOB JOCZ

'Priest against prophet, worldly church against the church of faith, the church of Aaron against the church of Moses — this is the eternal conflict in the church of Christ ...'

'Church of the priests against church of the Word, church of Aaron against church of Moses — this historical clash at the foot of Sinai, the end of the worldly church and the appearance of the Word of God, repeats itself in our church, day by day, Sunday by Sunday.'

(Dietrich Bonhoeffer: Sermon in Berlin, 28 May 1933)

The remarkable achievement of the Anglican communion is its ability to contain within its folds opposing theologies without open schism. The founding of Wycliffe College, whose centenary we are celebrating in this volume was, in fact, the result of an intra-church controversy which, though the drama was played out within the diocese of Toronto, went far beyond its boundaries.

The story of Wycliffe cannot be told without frequent reference to Trinity College which served, though unintentionally, as the *casus belli*, and these two colleges represented a deeper split which sharply divided the Church of England in the motherland in the second half of the nineteenth century.

THE TWO CAMPS

The Church of England in the nineteenth century was spiritually ill-equipped to meet the challenges of the age. Morally it was not in a position to provide strong leadership for the nation. Most of the clergy were poorly paid while bishops had exorbitant incomes. Absenteeism from parishes was prevalent. It has been estimated that three-fifths of the clergy in 1827 was non-resident. Nepotism was widely practised, the best livings being reserved for the sons and nephews of a few rich families. The church was unashamedly subservient to the state and did its bidding. Many of the church buildings were in disrepair and the services were dull. What Christian life there was derived from the evangelical revival and the Wesleyan movement; and in the background there was always the lure of the Roman Catholic church.

Resistance to Rome however was not only a matter of religious conviction but also of national pride. The Declaration Against Popery by oath was a requirement of all members of Parliament. It consisted of a denouncement of the Romish doctrine of transubstantiation, the mass, and the invocation of saints.

The term 'popery,' first coined by William Tyndale became a by-word for Englishmen. 'No popery' was the slogan of the mob, frequently ignorant of whether popery was a man or a horse. In 1631 when Parliament was summoned to Oxford, the slogan on the ribbons worn by the crowd was: 'No popery, no slavery!' Fear of popery was and still is an English obsession and this fact must be borne in mind when we deal with division within the church.

Yet English Christianity seldom spoke with one single voice. The Act of Uniformity in the year 1662 was unable to silence diversity of opinion regarding salvation, church, and ministry. There was a running dialogue between the church as established by law and the dissenters. The classical example is Richard Hooker's learned effort to deal with Puritan scruples. With the rise of Methodism the controversy shifted from outside to within the church itself. The later evangelical revival intensified the exchange of views and added fervour to the discussion.

Traditionally, the Church of England was about equally divided between High Church, Broad Church, and Evangelicals. The High Church party is sometimes described as latitudinarian in church discipline and legalistic in conformity to the establishment. It was always suspicious of 'ecclesiastical tinkers,' those restless spirits pressing for change.

The eighteenth-century evangelical movement, on the other hand, was essentially the result of a new emphasis upon 'personal religion.' Both Wesley and Whitefield had a passion for souls. There was little sympathy among stodgy churchmen with the enthusiasm generated in the revival meetings. Six students were expelled from St Edmund Hall, Oxford, in 1768, for having 'too much religion.' The peculiar emphasis upon experience frightened the establishment founded upon liturgical worship. George Every in his book, *The High Church Party: 1688-1718*, rightly intimates that men like Wesley and Whitefield would have given trouble to any church authorities. On the other hand, those touched by the revival dubbed established churchmen as 'High and Dry': without heat or fervour.

In between the two extremes were the Broad churchmen. Though the term was not used till a later date, it well describes those who refused to identify with either party and were content to call themselves 'Anglicans,' frequently in a purely traditional sense. When Broad churchmanship became theologically respectable it described those within the Church of England 'who took a broad and liberal view of the Anglican formularies and rubrics.' (Contributors to *Essays & Reviews* (1860) may be reckoned as Broad churchmen of this type.)

The different trends within the Church of England made for animated debate and resulted in an extensive literature. Thus far the debate was within the family which had much in common by way of tradition and history. The picture began to change with the appearance of the Oxford Movement (1833-45).

The avowed purpose of *Tracts for the Times* was to disseminate church principles both 'against Popery and Dissent.' The first tract was written by John Henry Newman and dealt in four pages with church policy and the apostolic succession. It was addressed to the clergy. Other tracts written by outstanding churchmen soon followed. These short leaflets gave way to learned and lengthy treatises of which the best known is Tract 90 also by Newman and dealing with the Thirty-nine Articles.

This tract marks the breaking point in Newman's theological position with respect to the question of transubstantiation. Dealing with Article 28 of the Thirty-nine Articles, he was driven to the conclusion that 'the change of the substance of Bread and Wine' denied by the article does not deny *every kind* (his italics) of change 'but opposes itself to a certain plain and unambiguous statement ...' Newman was motivated in re-interpreting this article by a need to defend the Church of England. It as yet involved no retraction of his own loyalties. He wrote: 'If Rome is to be withstood, it can be done in no other way.'

Reaction to Tract 90 was instantaneous. He was accused of '*evading rather than explaining*' the sense of the Thirty-nine Articles, and 'reconciling subscription to them with the adoption of errors which they were designed to counteract ...' This was the verdict of the heads of houses at Oxford. Subsequent events proved them right. When Newman and some of his followers seceded to Rome, Anglo-Catholicism came under suspicion of subversion. (This suspicion has never really subsided among evangelicals. Read, for example, the works of Walter Walsh, *The Secret History of the Oxford Movement* (1898), followed by *The History of the Romeward Movement of the Church of England: 1833-1864* (1900). The author, having explained that he writes 'from the standpoint of an Evangelical Churchman,' concludes by saying: 'To secure musical services, and histrionic performances, by a sacrifice of our Christian liberty to priestly bondage, is at best a poor bargain.')

For evangelicals, Anglo-Catholic theology constitutes a challenge to the basic Reformation principles. They see in it an effort to substitute the church for the Bible. Emphasis upon church means the authority of the priest and the power of the sacraments. It means apostolic succession as a condition of salvation. It means the layman's utter dependence upon priestly absolution. Evangelicalism must be understood as assertion by the layman of his rights against the encroachment of priestcraft.

Evangelicals opposed Anglo-Catholicism not only on theological grounds but also for national reasons. Anglo-Catholic leaning towards disestablishment, and its consequent leaning towards Rome, threatens the evangelical as a move towards ultimate submission to papal authority. Bishop Knox, writing as an evangelical, assessed the situation in this manner: 'The essence of the Oxford Movement was an attempt to assert the existence of a corporate body, wholly clerical, possessing Divine Right to prescribe for the Nation its faith and worship.'

At stake was the competence of Parliament, which is the voice of the laity, to pronounce upon matters of religion. A totally clericalized church contradicted the basic suppositions of English society. Efforts to interpret Church of England doctrine to coincide with that of Rome was looked upon as a subterfuge to deceive the innocent. Evangelicals could manage to co-exist in the same church with a variety of churchmen, but they could not countenance traitors who, when they said church, meant Rome.

Evangelicals were angered most by the subversion of the English Prayer Book into Roman Catholic doctrine. W.G. Ward declared that he could in all honesty put his signature to the Thirty-nine Articles and at the same time affirm the whole body of Roman doctrine.

Others took the same position. The chasm between the two camps appeared to be unbridgeable.

THE TWO SCHOOLS

It was inevitable that the divisions which obtained in the English church should be transferred to the colonies, since England was the natural pattern of social and religious life for all Englishmen abroad.

Trinity College, Toronto, was the creation of the Established Church of England — what seemed to be the 'official' church in the colonies. John Strachan, the first bishop of Toronto, planned an Upper Canada university in which theology would be given pride of place. The hope for such a school of higher learning had already been expressed by Lieutenant Governor Simcoe as early as 1792. In 1827 Dr Strachan obtained 'a Royal Charter by Letters Patent under the Great Seal,' whereby the Province of Upper Canada was granted the right to a College 'with the style and privileges of a University ... to be called King's College.' Unfortunately, things did not work out to the bishop's liking. The charter made no provision for religious tests and only professors were required to subscribe to the Thirty-nine Articles.

The University of King's College was officially opened 8 June 1843. It was planned to be 'thoroughly English in tone and style' with religious instruction only 'according to the Church of England.' But these restrictions met with opposition from the other denominations. In January 1850 King's College was transformed into the University of Toronto and all teaching of religion was abolished. Bishop Strachan felt deeply about education divorced from religion. 'The Church,' he said, 'ought to do nothing by halves. Her University must comprise an entire system of education, based on religion. Every branch of knowledge cherished at Oxford and Cambridge must be carefully and substantially taught ...' To do this Trinity College was founded in 1852. It comprised a university with a divinity school built into its charter, and the Diocesan Theological Institution at Cobourg which had been training Anglican clergy since 1842 was transferred to Trinity as its faculty of divinity.

The provocation which led to the founding of Wycliffe College was ostensibly the infiltration of tractarian teaching at Trinity. The person who took the brunt of the blame was the scholarly and eloquent provost, George Whitaker. The first rumblings came from Bishop Cronyn of Huron who expressed disquiet about certain doctrines being inculcated in the minds of young divinity students, such as reservation of the sacrament for the sick, exaltation of the Blessed Virgin Mary, prayer of the departed saints for those still living, seven sacraments instead of two, a Romish interpretation of the Eucharist, and the doctrine of baptismal regeneration. All these contentious subjects were hotly discussed in England and the secular and church papers were filled with accounts of lawsuits in which clergymen were accused of breaking the law of the land. The reaction on the part of the bishop of Toronto to such accusations can be gauged from his remark that Cronyn's objections would be 'better for a political agitator than a Bishop.' Provost Whitaker addressed two open letters to the bishop of Toronto in 1860 denying all allegations: He did not teach Mariolatry; he did not teach transubstantiation. What he taught was in accordance with the ancient Fathers, as well as the Anglican divines of the Church of England. But the denials did not allay Cronyn's misgivings. In an address to his clergy and laity the bishop maintained that he regarded Whitaker's teaching 'as a dangerous tampering with the false doctrine of the Church of Rome, directly leading to idolatry.' Citing a previous pastoral, Cronyn printed in italics for emphasis: '*As I cannot in my soul approve of the theological teaching of Trinity College, I believe that my appearing to sanction this teaching would be a positive evil.*'

In vain did George Whitaker try to explain in greater detail his position by publishing six lengthy articles in the *Dominion Churchman*, the official organ of the Church of England in Canada. The first appeared 11 July 1878, the sixth and last on 15 December in the same year. The stigma of Romanizing stuck to him to the end of his career.

Whitaker's articles are of considerable interest for they reveal the difficulties that arise when people talk at cross purposes. The heading for each of these articles was touchingly eirenic: 'The Duty of Mutual Toleration by Parties within the Church.'

The provost saw the cause of division as coming largely from imprecise use of words. The evangelicals, he thought, harped upon the word 'Protestant' when, in fact, they only meant sectarian theology which had developed since the Reformation. A condition for mutual toleration would require careful definition of terms. However, Whitaker was not prepared to give way on matters of faith and practice. He had already said in his open letter: 'I feel that it is due to the Church, to the College, and to myself, to show that I have not been guilty of raising needless points of debate, and that I cannot rightly or reasonably promise to modify my teaching for the future.' He reiterated that no compromise was possible in matters of faith.

All one could ask for was 'a wise and charitable abstinence from insisting on that which our Church does not call upon us to accept as revealed truth.'

A much harsher note was struck by the editor of the *Dominion Churchman* who took to task those who were 'setting themselves up in opposition to the Bishops' and, 'ignoring the Synods of the Dioceses, constitute themselves teachers, though ignorant of Church doctrine.' The writer disclosed that the 'pernicious errors' of these so-called churchmen was in fact Puritanism. The editorial was written under the heading: 'Hooker on the Grace of the Sacraments.' The paragraph in question consists of some 130 words with many inserted commas, until at last it reaches a full stop! This gives some indication of the temper in which it was written.

The occasion for the editorial is only too obvious: a year before, almost to the day, nine young men had sat down in St James' Schoolhouse for their first lecture in theology and thus initiated the institution now called Wycliffe College.

A.N. Bethune was emotionally involved in the controversy as a former professor of Trinity College and also as the diocesan bishop who naturally resented the agitation which divided the church. How he felt about the new school we can surmise from his last speech to synod, for he died soon afterwards while on a visit to England. The lengthy passage is headed: 'Our Unhappy Divisions' and covers almost four pages.

'There are, doubtless, faults of temper and misrepresentation,' he writes, 'on either side,' but he deplores the insinuations wherewith 'true and honest Churchmen' are being accused of leanings towards Rome. Good and honest men are 'tinctured with the errors of Popery' merely for being 'High Churchmen.' Their opponents shout 'the Church is in danger' without giving reasons for their apprehension. They accuse of sacerdotalism, ritualism, and sacramentalism those who venerate the sacraments, the priesthood, and Holy Scriptures. The bishop regrets the excesses in ritual which have occurred in the motherland, but this hardly applies to the colony. He regards the complaints of 'wilful and unreasonable men' who clamour for 'the cold, lethargic, barren days of half a century ago,' as utterly ridiculous. Their objections to the exhibition of the cross, painted windows, the chanting of the liturgy, surpliced choirs, and the solemn raising of the offertory plate, stem from ignorance, for these things have been practised without opposition for centuries. He appreciates the innovations which resulted in 'appropriate arrangements and seemly ornaments ... to the devout and reverential, and yet hearty manner of conducting the worship of God.' He is thankful for the Reformation of the sixteenth century, but its purpose was not to break the continuity with the Apostolic church.

The bishop ended his speech with a plea for 'mutual respect and forbearance' despite differences. The plea for toleration came from both sides. Deploring the yearly dissensions that are witnessed at the Toronto Synod, one writer to the *Dominion Churchman* 5 July 1877 pleads 'Let the extreme party-men on either side control their feelings and let the sound Churchmanship of the great majority have more sway and more time allotted to them in all deliberations.' As regards the 'Training School,' he can see no necessity for such a school; let both parties be represented in the management of Trinity College. Trinity certainly made several efforts to accommodate the newly organized opponents, even to the extent of appointing a professor on its staff who was a declared evangelical. On the other side, the *Evangelical Churchman*, the rival journal founded by the evangelical party on 18 May 1876, made similar pleas for toleration within the church. But for the evangelicals 'toleration' meant freedom of expression and unrestricted yielding to the prompting of the Spirit. The creation of the 'Protestant Divinity School of Toronto,' later to be known as Wycliffe College, was in fact carried out on the crest of a great spiritual awakening resulting from a mission at St James' Cathedral. It is indicative of the difference between the two rival journals that while the *Evangelical Churchman* was carrying glowing accounts for many weeks of the mission and its leader, the Reverend W.S. Rainsford, the *Dominion Churchman* grudgingly inserted one little paragraph barely mentioning the event. It is noteworthy that there is hardly any mention of St James' in the pages of the *Dominion Churchman* for 1877. There is a long letter to the editor signed 'Churchman' in which the writer complains of the wave of evangelists from the USA arriving singly, in twos, or as whole companies, 'even females.' He feels troubled 'about unauthorized *Lay preaching*' since preaching of the Gospel is the prerogative of the 'ordained ministers of Christ.' His other concern is the shedding of 'old accustomed rules and ceremonies,' as is now happening at St James' to the degree that people are sitting on benches 'inside the communion railings,' almost touching the Holy Table, so that there is no room for kneeling. To make things worse, the minister was without a surplice, and instead of the Prayer Book extemporary prayers were offered in which laymen and dissenting ministers took part — and this from the reading desk. That is how 'Churchman' felt about the mission at the cathedral.

In view of the almost complete silence on the part of the journal in respect to the Rainsford mission at the cathedral, the letter by 'Churchman' could not have been printed without sympathy. But Mr Rainsford earns the editor's displeasure for yet another reason. He chides him for attending a ceremony of the laying of a cornerstone of a new building by a schismatic body — the reference is to the Reformed Episcopal church — specially in view of his association with the cathedral. The editorial concludes with the remark: 'Playing with Dissent may lead a man in one direction, and playing with Rome may lead him in another; but the disloyalty to his own Church is equal in both cases.'

It was one thing to train men for the Ministry however and quite another to persuade a bishop to ordain them. The *Dominion Churchman* took pleasure in the thought that ordination is the sole and exclusive privilege of the bishop who alone determines conditions and qualifications of candidates: 'no one ever questioned the Bishop's undoubted right' in this matter. This may look 'arbitrary, if you please,' even *ultra vires*, as some declare, but it is for the good of the church. If evangelicals appeal to the practice as it obtains in the mother country, they are mistaken, for there has never been a case of two schools in the same diocese preparing men for the ministry. Even St Aidan's, Birkenhead, the new college founded in opposition to St Bee's, moved to another diocese.

This episcopal prerogative was contested by one speaker at synod who called for a new canon for bishops to the effect that bishops be bound to ordain any candidate properly qualified. The editor's reply on behalf of the bishop was to refuse 'to recognize, in any way whatever, the new institution — either to ordain from it, or to license any who had been ordained from it by any other bishop.'

Things, however, worked out differently. Bishop Bethune died soon after synod, and the new bishop, Arthur Sweatman, in his first charge to synod in June, 1878, declared himself an evangelical. He explained: 'a true Bishop of the Church,' must not allow himself to be 'the Bishop of a party.' Nonetheless, he continued, 'I claim that *I hold views* (his italics); and views of a very distinct character ... I hold most strongly the Protestant Evangelical views of our Reformed Church, as opposed to the sacerdotal and sacramentarian views which are characteristic of Rome.' He proudly declared himself a 'sound conservative Evangelical Churchman' dedicated to Reformation principles. He believed that 'the great bulk of our laity is staunchly, jealously Protestant.' But his intention was not to divide the Church: 'In the name of peace and Christian Charity, let us agree to forswear the use of invidious party names and cease to cast in each other's teeth the reproach of "High Church" and "Low Church" and know one another as fellow members of one and the same beloved Church.'

The bishop's counsel prevailed. In the end a compromise was reached. 'The Evangelical Association,' the militant centre of the Evangelical party, which carried on the struggle for Reformation principles, chiefly as a result of its occasional papers distributed widely in the diocese of Toronto, was to be disbanded. The new divinity school was to continue its operation. The *Evangelical Churchman* was to limit its publication to the local area.

The moderating influence of Bishop Sweatman, and the resignation of Provost Whitaker, relieved the tension to the extent that the Board of Management of the new school seriously considered amalgamation with Trinity College. At the instigation of the bishop a resolution was presented to the corporation of Trinity College suggesting the merger of the two schools on condition that: (a) the new provost be a person acceptable to the bishop; (b) an additional theological chair be established for the present principal of the Protestant Episcopal Divinity School; and (c) there be equal representation of evangelicals on Trinity's governing council. The board even offered to provide the salary for the new chair. The resolution did not meet with the approval of all the members. The treasurer of the Board, W.H. Harland, resigned; and another member, Robert Baldwin, put in a vigorous protest. The attempt at union failed over the appointment of the provost, when Dr Lobley, a man not approved by the bishop and not acceptable to the evangelicals, was chosen by Trinity Council. From the additional notes inserted in the official *Jubilee Volume of Wycliffe College* and deposited in the college library, it appears that each side blamed the other for the failure.

The advertised syllabus of the new school was an impressive document. The *Evangelical Churchman* commenting on the necessity for such a school explained that the need of the church was an educated clergy, adding: 'If we are to have an Evangelical ministry, we must have an Evangelical school in which they shall be trained.'

The full course of study occupies three years, each year comprising three terms:
1 / Michaelmas Term — From October 1st to December 15th (inclusive)
2 / Lent Term — From January 10th to Palm Sunday
3 / Easter Term — From Easter Tuesday to June 10th

Course of Study

First Year
1 / Hebrew begun
2 / Contents, origin, and character of the books of the Old and New Testaments
3 / Gospels and Acts in Greek
4 / Principles of Interpretation
5 / Paley's Evidences
6 / History of the Apostolic Church
7 / Homiletics
8 / Thirty-nine Articles, English and Latin Text, with Scripture proofs
9 / Elocution

Second Year
1 / Catholic Epistles and Apocalypse
2 / History of the Post-Apostolic Church to the Reformation
3 / Pearson on the Creed
4 / Thirty-nine Articles, with Boultbee
5 / Butler's Analogy
6 / Hooker, Book V; Jewell's Apology
7 / History of the English Prayer Book
8 / Homiletics (continued)
9 / Hebrew (continued)
10 / Elocution (continued)

Third Year
1 / Pauline Epistles
2 / Septuagint
3 / Reformation and the Church of England
4 / Thirty-nine Articles; Browne
5 / Pastoral Theology
6 / Composition and Delivery of Sermons
7 / Liturgics (continued)
8 / Hebrew (continued)

THE MAN ON THE SPOT

At this point the story of Wycliffe College becomes inextricably intertwined with the story of the man who for 28 years served as its first principal.

Reflecting upon the remarkable life of James Paterson Sheraton, the anonymous author of *In Memoriam* writes: 'It is almost impossible to express in fitting terms the greatness of debt owed by Wycliffe College and by evangelical churchmen all over Canada to Dr Sheraton's untiring zeal and devotion in the great cause for which Wycliffe was established. The personality of the College was the personality of the man, truly great in his real love and sympathy for the individual.'

Those who knew him personally, as did Dr H.J. Cody who was one of his students and later his colleague, regarded him as the 'builder of Wycliffe.' This he was in more senses than one. In the physical sense, he built the college several times over; in the metaphorical sense he erected an institution which has survived the storms of a century and is still full of life and vigour.

James Paterson Sheraton was born in the city of Saint John, N.B., 29 November 1841. He derived his given names from his maternal grandfather, Dr James Paterson, who was for half a century principal of the grammar school at Saint John and was regarded as one of the most distinguished scholars of the Maritimes. It was under the supervision of his grandfather that young Sheraton started his scholastic career. Long before his grandson was old enough to become a scholar at the grammar school Dr Paterson had instructed him in a variety of subjects, with special attention to science and Hebrew.

Sheraton graduated from the University of New Brunswick at the age of 20 with honours in Classics and Natural Science and with the Douglas gold medal. In preparation for the ministry he continued his studies under the private direction of the bishop of Fredericton, John Medley, and at King's College, Windsor, N.B. Medley had a modifying influence upon young Sheraton which served him later in good stead. He always spoke of the bishop who ordained him with true affection. This is the more remarkable as the bishop was not only a high churchman but the leading tractarian of the time.

Yet John Medley, who was consecrated bishop in May 1845 and became Metropolitan in 1879, was widely known and respected for his charity and moderation. Professor Eugene Fairweather of Trinity College has described him as the 'Tractarian Patriarch.' The eirenic spirit of Christian charity displayed by the bishop must have served as a wholesome restraint on the young principal of the newly founded institution when he discovered that in Toronto he was surrounded by two embittered and still fighting camps. Though a fervent evangelical who would never compromise on principles, Sheraton was anything but a bigot.

The *Mail and Empire*, acknowledged this, when it wrote on 25 January 1906 of Sheraton: 'A divine without bigotry, a scholar without pedantry, he was a model head of an institution established as a nursery of evangelical churchmanship. Gentleness and energy, two qualities rarely occurring together in the same personality, he possessed in a remarkable degree.'

Sheraton was ordained to the diaconate by Bishop Medley in December 1864 and to the priesthood a year later. He first served in several missionary parishes and when the living of Pictou, N.S. became vacant, he was appointed rector of the parish. It was during those years of parochial responsibility that young Sheraton began to lay the foundations of the great learning which served him well as principal of a theological institution.

As witness to his quite unusual scholarship we have the testimony of the bishop of Toronto. In his address at the funeral service in Wycliffe Convocation Hall, he said of Sheraton: 'With the exception of Dr. Body, the late Provost of Trinity College, he was the best Hebrew scholar among the members (of the Examining Board) and he exhibited the widest and most intimate acquaintance with the current theological literature of the day, both German and English. His reading must have been most wide and was always up-to-date.' Bishop Sweatman could say this from personal observation as he served with Sheraton on the same examining board for some fifteen years. There is also the testimony of others who expressed amazement at his great scholarship and wide reading, not only in theology and biblical studies but in the natural sciences, classical literature, and philosophy. He was apparently an accomplished botanist. Dr Cody speaks of him as a 'walking theological encyclo-paedia' who managed to combine his extensive biblical knowledge with a remarkable proficiency in science and other disciplines. In spite of Sheraton's scholarly bent he remained a practical man who displayed great organizing powers.

When called to Toronto to act as principal of the Protestant Episcopal Divinity School, there was no school, no organization, no faculty, no library. There was nothing, except a few eager students and the goodwill of many laymen. All the organizing, all the building, was undertaken by this physically diminutive man who was affectionately known as the 'little Doctor.'

Dr Cody, who writes of his 'old teacher, revered colleague and beloved friend' with obvious reverence, describes Sheraton's appear-ance as of small stature and delicate frame. He was bald-headed, bewhiskered, with thick spectacles, ruddy cheeks, and a cheery smile. Others have remarked on his frail constitution. It is therefore the more notable that the 'little Doctor' had such an inexhaustible supply of energy. In addition to his teaching duties, administrative responsibilities, and personal oversight of each student under his care, not to mention his incessant reading, he managed to find time to act as a member of the governing body of Ridley College at St Catharines, Ontario; as president of the Toronto branch of the Lord's Day Alliance; as vice-president of the Evangelical Alliance; as vice-president of the Upper Canada Bible Society; and to serve on the Board of Examiners for divinity degrees in the ecclesiastical province of Canada. He was also a member of the Senate of the University of Toronto and attended meetings most regularly. His contribution as a member of the Senate was generously acknowledged by his peers. The Senate not only attended his funeral in a body but the minutes contain the following citation:

> The Senate records its appreciation of his inspiring labours and unflagging interest in University education, his courage in supporting the views that he held, his punctual attendance at all academic gatherings where the well-being of the University could be promoted. Recognizing that it will not be easy to fill the place of a leader so many-sided, and so devoted to duties, the Senate can only express its sense of the loss which Wycliffe College has sustained. But the loss is more than that of Wycliffe College.

In addition to all his many labours, Sheraton edited the *Evangelical Churchman* for a number of years; he was also active as expositor of biblical material for Sunday school teachers, and managed to produce a number of theological booklets. He was engaged in writing a major theological treatise, unfortunately never completed, at the time of his premature death of heart failure at the age of 64. The Register of Burials at the Church of the Redeemer (Toronto) gives the cause of Sheraton's death as 'overwork.' This is probably the correct diagnosis.

To his literary and academic achievements must be added his organizing ability. He was a born builder.

On 1 October 1877, when nine men entered the door of St James' Schoolhouse and went upstairs to what was then the infant class room to meet their leader, the Rev J.P. Sheraton, they could hardly foresee the imposing edifice which now stands on the south side of Hoskin Avenue. Within five years, with the help of numerous friends and benefactors, the new college moved out of St James' School-house to a new building on College Street. Judging from photographs, it was an imposing building of red brick, with brown stone dressing and in scholastic Gothic style. In addition to lecture rooms and the usual offices, there was space to house the principal, the matron, servants, and 20 students. The report on this achievement ends with the remark: 'this elegant building cost $21,000 and is entirely free from debt.' The last statement is indicative of the enthusiasm and generosity of many lay people who supported the new school. The building was officially opened on 24 October 1882. The date was hailed as a red letter day.

The increase of students was such that by 1885 additional space became necessary. Thanks to the generosity of the Hon. Edward Blake, who donated $10,000, a new library and additional class-rooms were added. Samuel Hume Blake, vice-chancellor of Upper Canada, remained a staunch and generous friend of the college to the very end. There were other outstanding laymen who espoused the cause of Wycliffe and acted as benefactors such as Sir Casimir Gzowski, K.C.M.G., the Hon. Chief Justice Draper, C.B., Professor Daniel Wilson, president of the University of Toronto, the Hon. James Patton, Q.C., ex-vice-chancellor of the University of Toronto, and many others. But even this expansion proved insufficient. Another move became necessary and the present site on Hoskin Avenue was a judicious choice since it brought Wycliffe College right into the heart of the university.

The foundation of the new building was laid in 1890 and by the autumn of 1891 the building was finished. It says something of the visionary expansiveness of the 'little Doctor' who in an address to the alumni on 7 October 1891, when the college had barely settled in its new quarters, said: 'I hope before very long to see an extension to the south, with a front towards University College, providing additional dormitories, and a convocation hall which shall supply more adequately the accommodation for public gatherings ...'

Sheraton was as good as his word: 'Within two years a new library and a spacious Convocation Hall was erected. Housekeepers' apartments were built; the residential section was extended.' This building underwent further extensions after Sheraton's death but most of it was completed while he was principal.

We have already indicated that Sheraton's interests encompassed a large field. He was a born educator. His friends regarded him as a compulsive lecturer, excelling in biblical exegesis and systematic theology. Canon Cody describes him as 'a master in the art of teaching.'

George M. Wrong, who was one of Sheraton's students and later his colleague on the staff for about ten years, says of his principal that 'he lectured incessantly, persistently.' He describes Sheraton as a leading figure in the educational life of Toronto, 'a power in the Church of England, the centre of a busy Theological School, every part of which was dominated by his personality and felt the impulse of his convictions.' Though of small physique, small voice, and with no special gifts in oratory, this man who was shy in public gatherings outside the college walls was a most impressive figure on his home ground. Wrong expresses puzzlement at the apparent paradox in Sheraton's personality: 'there was a certain Hildebrandine determination in the gentle and retiring scholar, and he would have it his own way.' Friends urged him to devolve some of his duties on others and ease his burden in the management of the college but he could not do it: 'Dr. Sheraton was wedded to Wycliffe College and claimed the full right of a bridegroom.' To his description of his former principal, Wrong adds in a eulogy published in the University of Toronto Monthly in March 1906 the interesting observation that Sheraton's martyrdom was self-imposed and that he would not have had it otherwise: 'He found his chief joy in spending himself for the task which he was sure God had given him to do.'

With all of Sheraton's dedication to the task of training men for the ministry, he never lost sight of his Christian responsibility for the world outside. In spite of his many and onerous duties he still found time to conduct a Greek Bible class for university students on Sunday afternoons. William Stewart Wallace in his history of the University of Toronto describes him as a 'beautiful character who exerted at times a salutary influence in the councils of the University.' This is a touching description of a man whom many thought to be the cause of dissension in the church. The same writer asserts that 'Principal Sheraton,' was a 'man of gentle and truly Christian spirit.' This eirenic trait in Sheraton's character is corroborated by others. The *Mail and Empire* in an obituary notice wrote: 'Instead of more widely sundering the two shades of opinion within the Church as it was feared he might do, Principal Sheraton has helped Church of England men to forget that there ever was a serious cleavage.' The same writer went on to observe that 'by his fellowship with clergy of other Churches, and his help in the joint work of the Churches, he did something to deepen the sense of common Christianity and thus facilitated union.'

This ecumenical attitude on the part of Sheraton extended beyond theology to the other disciplines. He once wrote: 'Unfortunately, the medieval study of theology was cast in a very narrow mould, and it was too frequently placed in a position of antagonism, or, at least, of dictatorial dogmatism, towards the humanities, to its own grievous loss, as well as to the great injury of liberal education.' This revealing passage sheds light upon Sheraton's position regarding the function of a university. It was to be a place of higher learning where the various faculties co-operated for the ennobling of human life. He regarded medicine, law, and divinity as the three essential disciplines indispensable for ordered existence in society: 'the three great professions upon whose character and efficiency the well-being and progress of the community are so largely dependent.'

It was this conviction which prompted him to defend the independence and unity of the university. Thanks to his influence, Wycliffe College was looked upon as a 'bulwark' when the question of federation of the colleges became a burning issue. In a memorandum submitted to the Senate of the University of Toronto on behalf of Wycliffe College in 1897 Sheraton chides Dr Burwash and Victoria College for the decision to duplicate the university programme and thus weaken its unity: 'The people of Victoria shut themselves out of University College by their duplication of its work in Arts. This duplication was unnecessary, for the whole State Institution was open to them, and the State was bound to make provision for all their students in the provision of a complete Arts Course.'

Sheraton is described as 'a thorough-going but discriminating liberal' in politics and this bent of mind spilled over in his attitude to education. As far as Sheraton and Wycliffe were concerned, there was no need for a multiplication of 'sectarian' schools which would divide the academic community. The memorandum asks why students who already share classes in natural and physical sciences, in philosophy, history, Italian, Spanish, etc., cannot also share classes in Greek, Latin, Hebrew, French, German, and ethics? The issue arose in connection with the allocation of fees which it was feared would work out to the detriment of the university.

Sheraton's position regarding secular higher education is interesting as it throws light upon the question which led to the creation of a university separate from King's College. On 26 February 1818,

Bishop Strachan petitioned the House of Assembly of Upper Canada for a grant to aid theological education. The King's College charter of 1827, which gave power to confer degrees in divinity, made no provision for a distinct theological faculty. Philosophy and theology were to be taught together and were assigned to a single chair covering moral philosophy and divinity — both to be taught with a strong Anglican bias. This Anglican exclusiveness of King's College raised objections on the part of the other churches. The Church of Scotland in Upper Canada in particular pressed for a professorship in theology for the Presbyterian church at King's College. In 1837 a select committee of the Legislative Council approved the proposal of the British House of Commons that a professor in theology of the Church of Scotland in Upper Canada be appointed to teach at King's College. The college, however, took no action. To solve the problem of disunity, the House of Assembly recommended two years later that theological seminaries be established, one for each denomination. In the end, the Baldwin Act of 1849 abolished King's College and replaced it by the University of Toronto. This new development brought an end to theology as a part of a secular institution. But by an Act of 1853 denominational colleges were given the right of affiliation with the university. The Federation Act of 1887 completed the process of relating the theological schools to the University of Toronto.

Under Sheraton, the College applied for affiliation with the university and was granted the request by a statute of the Senate in 1885. This was confirmed by the governor-in-council. By the Act of the Ontario legislature in 1889 Wycliffe thus became a federated college and a constituent part of the University of Toronto. In the same year, after much delay, the Provincial Synod of the church passed a canon in respect to theological examinations. It accepted the Cambridge scheme suggested by Lightfoot and Westcott known as the preliminary examination for holy orders. By this canon Wycliffe became a recognized institution in the church, together with similar schools devoted to theological training.

The Senate of the University of Toronto appreciated Sheraton's exertions on behalf of the university and also his personal qualities as scholar and teacher. The degree of LL.D. was conferred on him in June 1896. Speaking at Convocation, the professor of comparative philology, Maurice Hutton, said:

This is not the place, nor am I the person, to eulogize Dr. Sheraton's work in his theological college. So far as that is concerned everyone who knows Dr. Sheraton knows that he is zealous in the cause of what he deems to be true religion, with a zeal not unworthy of that early master of Balliol, that uncompromising and fiery spirit concealed in a frail and emaciated frame, who is the hero eponymous and patron saint of Wycliffe College. But the University of Toronto knows another Dr. Sheraton, and it is the other Dr. Sheraton that it honours here to-day; the friend of university education in all its branches, the resolute member of Senate who has faced heavy responsibilities in the service of the university and has discharged those responsibilities at costs: in a word, the Churchman who has been not less zealous for useful learning than for sound religion.

The respect which Sheraton earned from his colleagues and peers was well summarized by the president of the university, James Loudon, professor of physics:

I should like to add a word expressing my appreciation of his personal character. No one was bolder and more determined in public as the champion of a cause, and no one in private life more gentle, unassuming, and amiable. Above all things he was distinguished by his unswerving honesty of purpose and his intense enthusiasm for the cause of right.

Perhaps Sheraton's greatest gift was his way with students. Wrong said of him that 'every student who entered the College he made his personal friend.' No wonder the college soon gained great popularity. By the year 1904 Wycliffe had graduated 150 students, most of them working in Canada. Thirteen graduates were engaged in mission work abroad. Fifty students were in course preparing for the ministry. It required $12,000 per annum to operate the school. Only one-third of this amount came from endowments; the rest was obtained from voluntary gifts.

Almost a full generation had passed since James Sheraton as a young scholar had undertaken the headship of an institution which in 1877 had been rich in promise but in little else. In the twenty-nine years of his regime, however, all the foundations of his college were well and truly laid. It had become a college in fact as well as in name, federated with a leading university, and located at the heart of its campus. It had become a training centre fully integrated with the church, its graduates accepted for ordination and service throughout the country. It had attracted support from a large company of concerned people on both sides of the Atlantic. It had acquired buildings still in use today. It had given leadership in missionary service throughout Canada and overseas second to none among colleges throughout the whole Anglican communion. It had established itself on evangelical principles, but had avoided being locked into a sectarian compound intellectually. The Sheraton years were years of achievement.

The Rev. James P. Sheraton
principal, 1877-1906

Mrs J.P. Sheraton
first chatelaine of Wycliffe

The Rev. Thomas R. O'Meara
principal, 1906-1930

TOP
The Rev. Ramsay Armitage, principal, 1940-1959

BOTTOM
The Rev. Robert M. McElheran, principal, 1930-1939

TOP
The Rev. Leslie Hunt, principal, 1959-1975

BOTTOM
The Rev. Reginald Stackhouse, principal, 1975-

ABOVE
The first Wycliffe College

OPPOSITE
Dining . . .
. . . and whining

Some distinguished missionary bishops

LEFT
Bishop M.N. Abraham, South India

ABOVE
Bishop William C. White, Honan, China

ABOVE
Bishop Heber James Hamilton of Japan

RIGHT
Archbishop Isaac Stringer, Rupertsland

The Centennial Celebrations 1977

Archbishop Scott greets retired principal,
Dr. Ramsay Armitage

Malcolm Muggeridge receives an honorary degree

Archbishop Coggan addresses the gathering

The centennial dinner tables
at the Royal York Hotel, Toronto

Wycliffe becomes a historical site:
the Hon. William G. Davis, premier of Ontario;
the Most Rev. E.R. Scott, primate of all Canada;
the Rev. R.F. Stackhouse, principal of Wycliffe

Wycliffe faces its second century:
at the heart — in the chapel;
in the world — the present facade on Hoskin Avenue

Expansion

The Principalship of
T. R. O'Meara
1906-1930

THOMAS R. MILLMAN

Thomas Robert O'Meara, son of the Reverend Frederick Augustus and Margaret Dallas O'Meara, was born at Georgetown, Ontario, 16 October 1864. In 1867 the family moved to Port Hope where his father became rector of St John's Church and where most of his childhood was spent. After leaving high school he entered University College and Wycliffe College in 1883. Although he was unable to complete his arts course because of ill health, he graduated from Wycliffe in 1887. A correspondent described him that same year in the *Evangelical Churchman* of 22 September as 'a young man of more than average ability.' He was ordained deacon in 1887 and served as curate for a short time under the Reverend James Fielding Sweeney, later fourth bishop of Toronto, at St Philip's Church, Spadina Avenue. Not long after his ordination to the priesthood in 1888 he was appointed assistant to Canon Alexander Sanson at Trinity Church East and held that post for fifteen years. On Sanson's death in 1904 he succeeded as rector, but in 1906 he was chosen as second principal of Wycliffe College.

In the summer of 1906 when he moved into the principal's house at the west end of the college he came as no stranger; he had been thirteen years old when the Protestant Episcopal Divinity School was started in 1877 and he had often heard the project discussed in his rectory home by his father, one of the founders. He had taken his course in the new and attractive Wycliffe College on College Street and may have acted briefly as dean of residence. In the autumn of 1888 at the ripe age of twenty-four he was authorized to visit the Maritime provinces on behalf of the college and he there collected

$1,400 from 230 subscribers for the sustentation fund. In 1889 he was appointed financial secretary, a position he held concurrently with his work at Trinity East until he became principal seventeen years later. As financial secretary he was closely linked with all aspects of college life, particularly with its business administration, and he quickly won the complete confidence not only of Principal Sheraton but also of the trustees and the council. In 1893 together with W.J. Armitage he visited England and Scotland soliciting subscriptions. In November 1894 he accompanied Dr Sheraton to the Maritimes and addressed an evangelical conference in Saint John on the work of the Canadian Church Missionary Association of which he was secretary. In June 1896 he was appointed a trustee of the college and in that year on a second journey to England he collected $6,400 in cash and $5,000 in promises. At a trustees' meeting, 5 June 1899, he was thanked for his 'unwearied labours on behalf of the sustentation fund.' Again in the summer of 1900 he made a financial appeal in England. In 1901 he urged the publication of an illustrated booklet for publicity purposes and saw it prepared and circulated. In 1903 he was engaged full time by the college and went on a fourth trip to England, raising $4,000 in cash and promises. In the same year he was made a member of the executive committee of the college and he revisited the Maritime provinces. As he had now become rector of Trinity East, a new agreement had to be made with the parish, but this did not prevent him from making a fifth journey to England on Wycliffe's behalf.

When, on the death of Principal Sheraton on 24 January 1906, the trustees and council were faced with the task of appointing a successor, their first choice was Henry John Cody who had been teaching at Wycliffe since his graduation in 1893. Assistant at St Paul's Church, Bloor Street, he declined in order to become rector of St Paul's in the following year. Their second choice, T.R. O'Meara, was made, so it was reported in the *Canadian Churchman*, 15 March 1906, because they believed that he had, above all other qualifications, the ability 'to act as a guide and moulder of character.'

YEARS OF EXPANSION, 1906-15

In his letter of acceptance to N.W. Hoyles, president of the council, O'Meara wrote: 'May He in whom all fullness dwells ever give needed wisdom and grace for this mighty undertaking.' A mighty undertaking it was indeed. Registrations rose steadily: 74 in 1906-7; 93 in 1908-9; 110 (85 in residence) in 1910-11. Accommodation became increasingly inadequate. The first addition to the building in the O'Meara regime was made in 1908 — a new dining room and kitchen, a faculty room, and 26 student rooms. Construction came to a climax in 1911-12 when land to the east was acquired from the university for the erection of a new principal's residence and the Founders' Chapel, the cost of the latter being met by Margaret Lewis Gooderham. The former chapel was turned into a room for student meetings. The upper part of the former principal's residence was transformed into rooms for students; the lower part, with a large reception room, became, in 1919, the quarters of the dean of residence and is now the administrative centre of the college. After 1912 no further significant structural alterations were made in the buildings until after the jubilee of 1927.

When Dr Sheraton became ill in 1905 temporary changes in duties of members of the teaching staff had to be made and permanent appointments soon followed. Dyson Hague, then a London rector, came in to teach liturgics as he had done in earlier years and as he continued to do on a part-time basis during the whole O'Meara period. A man of strong opinions and strong character he is still remembered by older graduates for the dramatic manner in which he conducted services. H.J. Cody undertook the instruction in systematic theology, the former principal's special subject, and he taught until 1916 when he became too busy elsewhere to continue lecturing. A 27-year-old Oxford graduate, C.V. Pilcher, was employed in 1906 to assist Cody and to teach Greek Testament. Unfortunately ill health shortened Pilcher's first period of usefulness at Wycliffe and he had to withdraw after two years. W.T.T. Hallam (Wyc. 1904) succeeded Pilcher and soon occupied the chair of New Testament, continuing to do so until 1922. T.H. Cotton (Wyc. 1901) taught apologetics from 1906 to 1918. The principal assumed responsibility for the department of practical theology and gave instruction for the next twenty years. As the number of students increased, the strain on the teaching staff became greater, particularly as some were employed for part-time only. Relief came in the spring of 1910 with the hiring of W.H. Griffith Thomas, former principal of Wycliffe Hall, Oxford, who was given the chair of Old Testament (although his specialty was really systematics) but who also taught other courses as well. The accession of this well-known English scholar was welcomed not only by the college but also by American evangelicals.

The last member of the teaching staff to be added during the years of expansion was Howard W.K. Mowll, a 23-year-old Cambridge graduate, recently made a deacon, who came to Toronto in the autumn of 1913. At first he taught English Bible and tutored in patristics, but an important part of his work was a kind of chaplaincy to the institution, combined with duties as dean of residence. Later he taught ecclesiastical history. Mrs Miriam Brown instructed in reading and voice culture in 1906 and was still teaching in the Jubilee year, 1927. Miss Amy Rogers was hired as assistant housekeeper in 1908 and was placed in charge in 1909, holding the post for over twenty years. She was important in the life of the college community and was invariably publicly thanked at the end of festive occasions in the dining hall.

The pattern of the academic year had already been set when O'Meara became principal. Graduation exercises were held at the end of April. At his first convocation, 27 April 1906, he was formally installed, presented with a licence by Bishop Sweatman and a certificate by N.W. Hoyles, president of the council. The re-opening of the college after extensive renovations in the following October coincided with alumni meetings. The bishop began proceedings by celebrating the Holy Communion and preaching. The Reverend Floyd Tomkins, rector of Holy Trinity Church, Philadelphia, conducted a quiet hour. At another event during the meetings Archdeacon George Exton Lloyd (Wyc. 1885), founder of the Barr Colony and later bishop of Saskatchewan, gave an address; at yet another the premier of the province was the guest of honour. Alumni members delivered a large number of brief addresses.

At the college closing in 1908 Convocation Hall was crowded, as it continued to be through the years on such occasions. At the combined college opening and alumni meetings in the autumn Sydney Gould (Wyc. 1893) told about his work as a medical missionary in Palestine, and several other speakers sounded the fundamental evangelistic note.

The history of the Literary Society, according to an account in the 1925 *Torontonensis*, ran parallel with that of the college. It originated in St James' schoolroom in 1877, moved to the College Street building, and finally to Hoskin Avenue where the first meeting was held in the common room in 1891. In O'Meara's first year as principal this venerable organization, then called the Wycliffe Literary and Theological Society, held a successful literary and musical evening in Convocation Hall in November. The *Wycliffe College Magazine* began publication in January 1913, and photographs of the editorial staff appeared regularly in *Torontonensis* until 1920.

The first annual field day conducted by the newly formed Wycliffe College Athletic Association was held on the university athletic grounds, Devonshire Place, on the afternoon of 6 November 1906. The occasion was graced with the attendance of the bishop of Selkirk, known more familiarly as 'Ike' Stringer (Wyc. 1892). The new principal was well aware of the importance of athletics in college life and emphasized the point in his first report to the council. Athletic colours were awarded at his first convocation.

The Wycliffe College Missionary Society, begun in 1881, was still active under O'Meara. Indeed, the principal had been secretary in his undergraduate days. Its purpose was to supply student services for vacant parishes and missions and to conduct evangelistic work in the city and suburbs. The 1904-5 report of the society tells that students were working in the summer in seven dioceses as far apart as Saskatchewan and Nova Scotia. Photographs of the executive of the society began to appear in *Torontonensis* in 1912. The *Jubilee Volume* of 1927 relates the splendid story of the achievements of the Missionary Committee of the Alumni Association of the college, its development into 'Wycliffe Missions' and then its amalgamation with the Canadian Church Missionary Association in 1895. After 1903 the spirit which had energized these earlier efforts manifested itself in the newly formed Missionary Society of the Canadian Church, and in this unifying task the hand of Dr O'Meara, long-time honorary secretary of the C.C.M.A., was clearly evident. The Canadian Church Missionary Society, as it was renamed in 1902, still maintained a separate life and held occasional public meetings, but its role was not as prominent as in earlier years. A Wycliffe association for laymen was formed in 1908 to foster an interest in and increase support for the college. Its life, however, was short.

From his appointment as principal in 1906 until the impact of World War I began to be felt in 1915 Dr O'Meara was an exceedingly busy man. (He had been awarded an LL.D. by the university in 1906 and was made a canon of St Alban's Cathedral by Bishop Sweeney in the same year.) Financial secretaries beginning with F.J. Lynch in 1906 and continuing with H.D. Raymond and A.L. Fleming were primarily charged with raising money for the college in Canada and elsewhere, but the momentum of O'Meara's long years in that pursuit continued, particularly on his frequent visits to England. On these occasions he maintained links with subscribers of past years, but he was now equally concerned with obtaining students for the college. The call for men to work in the north and west was then particularly insistent and the response of Canadians was not strong enough to meet the need. At this time he built up a close connection with the Colonial and Continental Church Society through its secretary, J.D. Mullins. For years the society offered to pay from £30 to £50 annually to men who studied in Wycliffe, for work in the northwest. By 1915 O'Meara had visited western Canada on four occasions. He was acutely aware of the need of men for the ministry in that vast area and gave enthusiastic support to those who volunteered to work there in the long summer vacations. He was also much interested in American theological institutions and in 1911 he visited seventeen of them in order to study their teaching methods. As his name became known he was called upon to give addresses and to join inter-church committees. In his report to the college council in 1910, for example, he related that he had addressed a students volunteer convention in Rochester and that he had been in New York in connection with preparations for the International Missionary Conference to be held in Edinburgh. He was also slated to speak at a conference in Halifax.

Relations with the university community were close. As principal, Dr O'Meara was an ex-officio member of the Senate, sitting in that body with two representatives of the college council, one of whom was always Dr Hoyles. His term as principal coincided largely with the presidency of Robert Falconer, later Sir Robert, and the two men were well acquainted. As Wycliffe men usually took their arts course in University College, strong ties bound the two institutions together at this time. Wycliffe's convocation hall was useful to the university from the first. In November 1907 an exhibit of Egyptian antiquities collected by C.T. Currelly was shown in the hall, and again in 1909 at Falconer's request the hall was used for six weeks for a similar purpose. After 1914 the official name of Sheraton Memorial Hall was given to it.

Relations with the University of Trinity College, as yet in its first old buildings on Queen Street, were frequently matters of concern. But by 1910 earlier antipathy between supporters of the two institutions had been lessened. The provost of Trinity attended the opening of the new Wycliffe convocation hall in 1902. A Trinity professor addressed the Wycliffe alumni in 1906 and a number of Trinity graduates were present on that occasion on the invitation of the principal.

In retrospect, the expansionist period from 1906 to 1915 was a kind of golden age for Wycliffe. The excellence of the work of the first principal and his devoted supporters was now being made manifest. Graduates in the worldwide mission field and in parishes across Canada were making the name of the college well known and respected at home and abroad. In the council minutes for 1901 it is recorded that the uniform and successful policy of the college from its foundation had been 'to go forward in the work depending under God upon the logic of events to compel recognition by the Church at large.' To a great degree that recognition had indeed been accorded. Dr O'Meara was able to report to the council in 1909 that the college enjoyed the confidence of a larger constituency than ever before in its history.

YEARS OF CONTRACTION, 1915-20

When the fall term opened in 1914 the college was completely filled and the graduating class of 1915 was the largest ever, but the outbreak of war and its terrible continuance brought to an end the striking progress of preceding years. The *Telegram* reported, 5 October 1914, that the annual conversazione, the highlight of the students' year, had been cancelled, the money saved to be given to Belgian relief or to the unemployment fund of the city of Toronto. The Literary Society decreed that every man should join the University Rifles or take up Red Cross work. By April 1917, 52 students and 30 graduates had enlisted, 2 were prisoners of war, 8 had been killed; only 44 students were registered in the college. Before the war ended, 14 members of Wycliffe College had died and 125 graduates and undergraduates had served in the armed forces in Canada and overseas. Two bronze tablets, and four stained glass windows in the chapel, commemorate them.

In no part of Principal O'Meara's correspondence is the secret of his influence more clearly shown than in a file entitled 'Men at the Front.' Letters from graduates and undergraduates flowed in to him from training camps in Canada and England, from prisoners of war in Germany, from chaplains, from hospitals, from somewhere in France, from Baghdad, Palestine, and Egypt. In these letters older men describe their experiences, younger men confess their frustrations and temptations, and all attest the strength of the fellowship which had been built up in the college and maintained in the stress of war. The principal's replies sometimes took the form of a newsletter, but always there were personal references. To some he gave fatherly advice and encouragement; to others news about their families, expressions of sympathy in their hardships, and pride in their achievements. To all he gave assurance that they were constantly prayed for and remembered. One in whom he took a special interest was A.C. Trivett who married his second daughter, Marian Catherine, 20 June 1917.

The use of the splendid new Hart House by members of the armed forces brought war exercises to the very walls of the college and to the campus and Queen's Park. The principal characterized these soldiers as, on the whole, very quiet and well behaved. 'I have no complaint to make of them' he wrote to Howard Mowll, 5 January 1917, 'apart from the fact that they sprinkle our lawn with cigar boxes, cigarette butts and whiskey bottles. I suppose, however, that this kind of thing is quite to be expected.' To a missionary he wrote, 16 February 1916, that it was 'strange and almost weird' to have the college so comparatively empty after those years of overflowing numbers.

Another development brought the war even closer to the college. *Varsity*, 21 November 1917 noted the event in the following lugubrious words:

The hush of midnight had fallen upon the halls of old Wycliffe. Not a light shone in the rooms or corridors. Not a student toiled at his nightly task. The stillness was the stillness of death. Wycliffe was passing away. As if from deep subterranean passages came the faint strains of 'The Dead March in Saul.' Louder it grew and fell on the ear the slow measured beat of the muffled drum. Led by the Dean in full academic costume, the funeral cortege, the casket borne by four weeping freshmen, passed in stately procession through the deserted halls...

The reason for this mock sorrow was the taking over of the east wing of the college by the Royal Air Force for the purpose of cadet training. Only the west wing and the chapel were left for the college. Writing to Walter Geddes, 23 November 1917, the principal remarked:

As we are in the midst of our transfer from being a quiet and orderly Theological College to our new role as a military barracks with two hundred and fifty flying men in it, you can easily understand there is not much quiet opportunity for letter writing.

Wycliffe was indeed under partial occupation until April 1919, but in the following October the building was re-opened for its original purpose after considerable renovation. Despite these unusual circumstances, academic life followed its usual routine. In April 1917, only 31 students were in attendance. In the spring of 1919 there were 33, but prospects were improving because of the end of the war and the return of a number of men from overseas. Changes in the teaching staff occurred with some frequency in this time of contraction. George Wrong (Wyc. 1883), one of the foremost Canadian historians, retired in 1915 after nine years of service and his work was taken over by Howard Mowll. Griffith Thomas, apparently never completely satisfied in his relations with the college, resigned in 1919 and moved to Philadelphia where a base for a broader ministry than was afforded in Canada was provided. He died in 1924. His work at Wycliffe was taken over by C.V. Pilcher who rejoined the staff as part-time lecturer in 1916. In 1918, T.H. Cotton resigned to become rector of St Aidan's Church. E.A. McIntyre replaced him at first in apologetics, but he had begun to teach systematic theology in 1919 and also taught church history for a time. A.L. Fleming succeeded H.D. Raymond (later rector of St Paul's, Charlottetown, and Archdeacon of P.E.I.) as financial secretary. J.D. Falconbridge and R.A. Hiltz (Wyc. 1904) joined the staff as honorary lecturers in church law and Sunday school methods respectively.

By an Act of the provincial Legislature in 1916, Wycliffe was given authority to confer degrees in divinity, a step which gave great satisfaction. The first honorary degrees of doctor of divinity were given in 1917 to Archbishop S.P. Matheson, Bishop J.F. Sweeney, and Bishop E.C. Acheson (Wyc. 1889). The first D.D. by examination was conferred on W.T.T. Hallam. In recognition of Wycliffe's standing, it became one of the four institutions to benefit from the Colonel R.W. Leonard Foundation which was set up in 1916 and enlarged in 1923.

During these years, members of the teaching staff were on the move during the long vacations and at other times. Mowll spent the summers of 1915, 1916, and 1917 in western Canada and travelled to eastern Canada as well. He visited graduates and was warmly received both as a preacher and as a missioner. He returned to England in 1917 hoping to obtain a chaplaincy, but was not successful until early in 1918. He saw service in France for six months and returned to Toronto in 1919, resuming his work in Wycliffe after an absence of two years. At first, Mowll found difficulty in adapting again to Canadian life, but he was encouraged and befriended by Dr O'Meara and is still remembered as a man of piety and ability. W.H. Griffith Thomas toured the Canadian west in

1916 and travelled in the United States in 1917 and 1918. W.T. Hallam spoke at a Northfield S.V.M. Conference in 1917 and visited the Maritimes in the same year. As has been noted, Dr O'Meara went west several times. His first automobile, provided for him by the college in 1918, made it more convenient for him to travel in the vicinity of Toronto.

Principal O'Meara's labours continued as constant as before despite the discontinuance of his journeys to England during the war years. Membership on the governing bodies of the Church of England Deaconess and Missionary Training House in Toronto, Havergal College, Toronto, and Ridley College, St Catharines, consumed time and energy. He was much concerned with the Araucanian Mission of the South American Missionary Society in Chile and corresponded frequently with Miss Louy Thomas, a Toronto friend and missionary, as well as with Charles Sadleir (Wyc. 1892), director of the mission. He had many contacts with the China Inland Mission and spoke at a C.I.M. Conference at Niagara in June 1916. His close connection with the Colonial and Continental Church Society led him to some involvement with Emmanuel College and with the Caron-Herbert Mission of that society in the diocese of Qu'Appelle. The mission, founded in 1909, was served by several Wycliffe men. He corresponded with missionaries in India and Japan, and with Canadian bishops who wanted men to occupy the mission stations during the summer. The strain of the busy years took their toll in the autumn of 1920 when he spent two and a half months in a sanitarium from mid-November until the following February.

POST-WAR YEARS AND JUBILEE

With the end of the war a number of men returned to take up their interrupted studies, and other registrations gradually increased: 38 in 1919, 65 in 1920, 72 in 1923. By the fall of 1926, every room was occupied by students preparing for the ministry. Again the former pattern of the principal's travels was resumed, voyages overseas every second year, 1922, 1924, 1926. In 1923 and 1925 he visited the Canadian northwest and in 1926 he went to the United States as well. The teaching staff saw a number of changes. In 1922 Professor Hallam, later to be bishop of Saskatchewan (and Saskatoon), retired after fourteen years service to become principal of Emmanuel College, Saskatoon. On his trip overseas in that year, Dr O'Meara engaged B.W. Horan of Trinity College, Dublin, as a replacement. In 1922 Howard Mowll left to be consecrated assistant bishop of West

China. In 1923 William Edington Taylor (Wyc. 1903), who had served briefly in 1902-3 as tutor in apologetics and missions, returned to the staff after long experience in the International Y.M.C.A. and the World Christian Student Federation, particularly in China. Professor McIntyre died, deeply mourned, after a long illness, in 1926. Thomas William Isherwood, a vigorous young Oxford graduate and a great favourite with Dr O'Meara, was his successor in the chair of systematic theology. R. Mercer Wilson, Trinity College, Dublin, joined the staff at the same time as professor of church history. A.L. Fleming (Wyc. 1916), later bishop of the Arctic, was followed as financial secretary by Sextus Stiles, then by John Blodgett.

In an address to the graduating class of 1918 Canon Cody advised the men to take their work tremendously seriously but not to take themselves too seriously. The postwar generation acted on his advice literally, approaching their studies with great determination and their college life together in a light-hearted manner. The *Varsity*, 27 October 1920, describes an initiation ceremony which took the form of a court in which freshmen were tried for committing various trumped-up offences and were given ridiculous penalties. The same newspaper on the following 11 December described a highly successful mock parliament:

> To the strains of 'Old Black Joe' the speaker of the House entered preceded by the mace and followed by court pages and functionaries. Business was begun immediately by the Labour member from Hogtown asking the Premier whether he could define the difference between Loew's Uptown and Pantage's Downtown. The Crown Minister ably responded and informed the member that one was low in name and other was low in nature.

The *Varsity* correspondent concluded with the comment: 'The only regret is that more parliaments were not like this. If they were, then "Government of the people, by the people, and for the people would vanish from the earth." '

Mock courts, parliaments, and even convocations continued for years to be cherished student traditions, but debates were conducted with appropriate dignity. Other annual activities were the cross-country run and the field day. The first athletic banquet, held in 1927, was addressed by Dr Cody. Other speakers were J.D. Trees, representing the council, Dr Hague of the teaching staff, and a student, L.M.M. Pepperdene.

Indication of a new spirit of unity in the church was made evident in the spring of 1921 when it became public knowledge that Dr Cody, one of Wycliffe's most distinguished graduates, had been offered, but declined, the post of provost of Trinity College. In June 1921 a further effort was made to unite the two institutions, but again no progress was made. In 1922-3 some Trinity students took lectures at Wycliffe as their own professor was ill. In 1925 a Toronto rector brought the Wycliffe-Trinity situation to public notice in a sermon which was given prominence in the press, but again nothing resulted.

The impact of the ecumenical movement was beginning to be felt in Toronto at this time. Discussion about a school of missions began in 1917-18 and the institution was finally set up in 1921. In 1919 the plan of co-operative theological teaching developed in Montreal was being considered in Toronto. Writing to Archbishop DuVernet, 12 December 1918, O'Meara remarked: 'This plan would not only secure the almost certain raising of the standard of theological education, but would give each College, including Wycliffe and Trinity, the opportunity of drawing more closely together in sympathy and co-operation.' Little progress was made along the lines forecast by O'Meara. It was not until the creation of the Toronto Graduate School of Theological Studies and particularly of the Toronto School of Theology in 1969 that such co-operation became a reality.

With the fiftieth anniversary of 1927 in mind bulletins began to be issued as early as 1925. A jubilee committee was set up and in May 1926 it reported to the council about the celebrations which were planned for September 1927. Two important decisions were made — to hold meetings not only in Toronto but also in other Canadian centres, and to provide a travelling fund for graduates and wives to enable them to attend from distant parts of Canada and the world. To give a keynote address at the celebration and to travel across Canada, the principal invited John Taylor Smith, bishop of Sierra Leone 1897-1902 and chaplain general of the British Army, 1902-25. As a result of these decisions and other careful planning, the jubilee was a huge success. The fact that it coincided with the centenary celebrations of the University of Toronto was also an advantage.

Three major events in Toronto deserve comment. The first was the jubilee convocation in the Convocation Hall of the University on 22 September 1927. About 250 graduates were in the procession. A section was allotted to wives of graduates, many of whom were present through the generous provision of the college. Representatives of church and state attended and brought greetings, and honorary degrees were conferred. It was indeed a memorable event.

The second was the jubilee service in St Paul's Church on Friday, 23 September when every seat in the great building was filled. Ten archbishops and bishops, 230 members of the clergy, Wycliffe students and staff, and representatives from sister institutions and from government attended. The choir of St Paul's assisted by the choirs of four city churches led in a triumphal *Te Deum* and sang the Hallelujah Chorus from Handel's *Messiah*. Bishop Taylor Smith's eloquent sermon graced the occasion. Bishop Sweeney pronounced the benediction.

The third occasion was the jubilee dinner in the Great Hall of Hart House, 26 September. Several speeches were made, one by the provost of Trinity, F.H. Cosgrave, who alluded to the attendance of Trinity men at lectures given by Wycliffe professors. Principal Vance (Wyc. 1905) of the Anglican Theological College of British Columbia reminded the guests that one of the greatest tests of the vitality of an institution was the spirit with which it could adapt itself to new truths. Dr Cody, chairman of the Board of Governors of the university, who had taught at Wycliffe for twenty years, said: 'I don't think any College can live on its past. The College really lives on two factors — first the strength and influence of its teaching staff, and, secondly, the strength, devotion and piety of its graduates.' Up to 1927 Wycliffe had 397 graduates, 75 in missionary service.

Writing to the council chairman, J. Shirley Denison, immediately after the major celebrations, O'Meara remarked:

The observance of the Jubilee of the College cost much in thought and labour over many months, as well as a considerable sum in money value, but I believe, even in a way of investment, it was all worthwhile. I do not think that anyone who was privileged to be present at one or all of the public gatherings — the Convocation, the Service at St Paul's or the closing dinner — will ever forget the sight or lose permanently the inspiration of those occasions. Never in my life have I been present at such a gathering as that in St Paul's Church, nor do I suppose I will ever have the opportunity again. The outstanding success of the Jubilee brings to us a great challenge for earnest effort and efficient service for the years to come.

At an 'At Home' given by the O'Mearas on the afternoon of 23 September 1927 a purse of gold was presented to the principal and a basket of flowers to Mrs O'Meara.

The involvement of Bishop Taylor Smith was a happy circumstance. Spiritually he was a devout Christian leader of vast experience. Physically he was a large man, so much so that the waves he raised when he plunged into the Hart House pool were the topic of amazed conversation on the part of those who witnessed the spectacle. He carried the inspiration of the jubilee to a number of nearby Ontario towns, conducted a mission in St Paul's, and then travelled west to Winnipeg, Saskatoon, Calgary, and Vancouver. He then turned east to Montreal, Quebec, Charlottetown, Saint John, and Halifax. He wrote to Dr O'Meara from Vancouver, 29 October 1927:

My Dear Principal:
Royal progress can only express the time I have had since last we met. Kindness, opportunity, privilege, pleasure, follow one another in quick succession. God has been most gracious in leading and blessing to individuals and communities. I have tried to lift up Jesus and the witness has been testified to by many.

The bishop, after a long and tiring itinerary sailed back to England in December. In connection with jubilee, T.W. Isherwood toured the north and the west, and C.V. Pilcher went to eastern Canada.

In 1928 a jubilee fund of $150,000 was initiated, the money to be used to build a new library and to make alterations and improvements in the main college building. Plans for a Blake Memorial Library had been laid as far back as 1913, but the war had put a stop to the project. The matter was raised again in 1924 as one of urgency by Professor McIntyre, the librarian, and by the principal in his annual report to council. It was finally envisaged in 1928 as an aim of the Thanksgiving Fund. In 1929 Colonel R.W. Leonard and Mrs Leonard of St Catharines gave $100,000 for this purpose and the new and handsome structure (in the dream of acting Principal Dr Taylor, the first unit in a completely new college) was opened on 22 April 1930. Reuben Wells Leonard, a council member from 1910 and vice-chairman in 1914, was one of Wycliffe's greatest benefactors. The library was but one of his many gifts.

Although the Edward Canfield Whitney Bequest matured after Dr O'Meara's death, he and S.H. Blake played the principal part in presenting Wycliffe's case to this wealthy and prominent businessman of Ottawa. E.C. Whitney had a great regard for Blake who died in 1914. Whitney died in 1924 but the bequest was not received until several years later when it had increased to about $700,000. It was the largest single gift received by Wycliffe in the College's entire history.

One further aspect of the jubilee was the decision to give Dr O'Meara leave of absence for a year to visit graduates throughout the world. The position of acting principal was given to Dr W.E. Taylor. The O'Mearas left Toronto in September 1928 and travelled first to England and Ireland. From there they crossed to the continent and thence to Palestine. Two months were spent in India, part of the time in the south, the home of the Mar Thoma Syrian church whose bishop had been educated at Wycliffe. The climate had a bad effect on Dr O'Meara's health but he proceeded to Shanghai where his son-in-law, A.C. Trivett, was dean of Holy Trinity Cathedral. Here he had a relapse but recovered sufficiently to visit Japan. The travellers returned to Toronto near the end of August 1929.

Canon C.H. Marsh, president of the Alumni Association, soon wrote to ask him to address the association at the forthcoming annual meeting. Dr O'Meara expressed his keen disappointment at being unable to do so and then proceeded:

> It is now forty-six years since I entered the doors of Wycliffe College as a humble freshman, and my love, loyalty and enthusiasm for the College and for the principles for which it has always so gloriously stood have grown and increased from that day until now. There never ... has been a period when I have been so proud of the College and of the men which it has, under God, been able to fit for foreign service as I am at the present moment. In spite of my indisposition, from which I am still suffering to some extent, I have been able personally to see every individual graduate upon my proposed list when I started a year ago, with three exceptions, and the political state of affairs in China during my time there utterly prohibited me from going up country to see them, or their coming down to Shanghai to see me.

Unfortunately the indisposition of which Dr O'Meara wrote made him unable to take up college duties at the beginning of the fall term. A few weeks spent in Florida failed to restore him to health and he died in Toronto on 10 January 1930.

Thomas Robert O'Meara was well fitted by his background and experience for the position he filled with distinction for almost 24 years. He learned from his parents the faith and patience necessary for missionary work as they told him about their long and often disappointing years before his birth among the Ojibways of Manitowaning. His older brother, J.D. O'Meara, who had gone to Winnipeg in 1872, as both a rector of a parish and teacher at St John's College, acquainted him with church affairs in Rupert's Land. It may be added that two more of his brothers were ordained — Charles, who served in Canada and in the United States, and Arthur, who worked in the Yukon and British Columbia. His years under Canon Sanson taught him about parish life. His familiarity with financial matters stood him in good stead as principal. He had the advantage of coming to the principalship at a time of rapid advance, but he was also fortunate in knowing personally many of the principal supporters of the college, both in Canada and in England, and he was able to preserve their loyalty and goodwill. He had the backing of many prominent business and professional men who served on the college council, particularly Samuel Hume Blake, and Newman Wright Hoyles, almost the last of the original founders of the college, who died in 1927. He maintained communication with graduates to an unusual degree, giving sound advice and encouragement to those who consulted him about their work and their problems. To undergraduates he was not a remote academic figure but one who understood their practical difficulties and frequently invited them to his home. His wife, Harriet Boyd, whom he married in 1889, a daughter of one of the college founders, aided him in dispensing hospitality to succeeding generations of students. His sound judgment led him to employ members of the teaching staff of good experience and of good promise, men who both at the college and in their life's work attained positions of honour and usefulness in the church. He had excellent administrative ability and managed the business and domestic affairs of the college with efficiency.

As the years passed and the college became known not only in Canada but outside the country's borders, O'Meara came to be a symbol of moderate Evangelical Anglicanism and to be widely accepted as a spokesman for this strong and vital element in the church. Bishops of missionary dioceses relied on the college to help them man their mission stations, particularly in the summer months. Dr O'Meara's copious correspondence illustrates the remarkable breadth of his interests and the extent of his influence. He was well regarded outside his own communion. When, for example, it was learned that he was about to make a world tour, he was asked by the United church to visit *their* foreign missions whenever it was possible.

He had a firm faith in the value of his vocation. When Charles H. Shortt returned from Japan in 1918 to take charge of a theological school in Vancouver, O'Meara wrote to his old acquaintance of Port Hope days:

My dear Charlie ... may you have great joy and blessing in your new work ... Although it has difficulties all its own, and I sometimes think greater than any other branch of ministerial work, yet after thirteen years of experience I would not change places with any Bishop or Archbishop or the very highest in the land.

To Jabez Gander (Wyc. 1886) who wrote to him in old age in pencil, with trembling hand, enclosing a small contribution to the college, O'Meara replied with loving simplicity, 5 November 1926:

My Very Dear Friend:
God is really blessing our work ... If only we can keep humble and loyal to Him there is no reason why the best days of Wycliffe should not be in the future rather than in the past.

Depression

The Principalship of R. B. McElheran

1930-1939

ALAN HAYES

R.B. McElheran's principalship (1930-9) spanned a period of crisis, both in society at large and in the church in particular, without precedent in the modern 'first world.' The Great Depression, first and foremost, produced horrifying material adversity and spiritual despair. Unemployment and physical misery challenged the Canadian church, which was still the country's principal social service agency, to care for the lonely and starving on a vast scale and to press for economic justice for the ordinary citizen; but the church was itself partially paralyzed by the bankruptcy of many of its investments and the exhaustion of many of its usual sources of revenue. Moreover, the Depression turned the values and ideals of previous generations topsy-turvy; it undermined the carefree lifestyles of the post-Victorian era; it shattered confidence in existing structures of government and finance. And the church itself was implicated in the ruin of the old systems — for it, too, as an Ontario priest named Henry R. Hunt (now Bishop Hunt) pointed out to a group of Wycliffe alumni in 1934, had 'tended to fall in line with the vested interests.' Canadians faced a special dimension of the Depression crisis in that they were now cutting the ropes which bound their country to its imperial moorings. Loyalties to England were dissolving; the mother country, itself facing financial and political chaos, could not rescue its beleaguered colony; Canada, with its own landscape and frontier, with its own two nations overshadowed by a powerful southern neighbour, was searching for an identity distinct from Britain's. Finally, the theological establishment, too, was being shaken. Barthianism, which had swept through Europe like a tidal wave after the World War I, was already lapping mildly at Canadian shores at the end of the 1920s. The implications of this new evangelicalism for conventional kinds of churchmanship were tremendous. It threatened, first of all, popular theological liberalism, with its hopes of human progress towards an earthly kingdom of God and its sentimentalized ethic of human brotherhood. It threatened Anglo-Catholicism, with its somewhat defensive claims for the authority of the institutional church and its rather esoteric emphasis on ecclesiastical ritual. And it also threatened the older evangelical school represented by Wycliffe College. Whereas the evangelical tradition of 1877 stressed God's influence on the individual human consciousness, Barthian evangelicalism saw God working above all in human community and in human history. Where the tradition maintained that doctrines and liturgical formulas enjoyed a once-and-for-all authority, Barthianism insisted that the Spirit continued to guide Christ's church and that God's purpose continued to be unfolded in the world. Whereas the tradition predicted God's activity in the future from his self-revelation in the past, Barthians allowed God to transcend the rules of human logic in His own surprising way.

Into this period of crisis came Wycliffe College with a peculiar problem of its own. The founders and original friends of the college, and even most of those who had known them well, had vanished from the scene; the college in which they had institutionalized their deepest faith now had to be entrusted to a new generation. Wycliffe, looking for new leadership, entering unfamiliar and even frightening territory, confronted by new theological thought, stood on the threshold of another era. It paused to find its bearings. To its new principal fell the task of steering a true course.

Robert Benjamin McElheran was born in London, Ontario, 1 February 1877. His father was first a newspaper publisher and editor, later an educator, and for more than thirty years secretary to the London Board of Education. His mother, a loving, religious woman, apparently had the stronger influence on Bob — or, as she alone called him, Robbie. When he confided in her, at age 10, that he had decided at a missionary meeting at their Anglican parish church to become 'a preacher, a fisher of men,' she supported him enthusiastically. Her death two or three years later came as a heavy blow to him from which he was slow to recover. He left high school before graduation and did chores for a weekly newspaper called the *Farmer's Advocate*. So creditable was his work that the newspaper promoted him to be its western accounts representative in Winnipeg, then a thriving railroad town of about 20,000 in the heart of the western frontier. The Anglican priests in his new parish were soon impressed with the devout and dedicated young man, and when in 1898 the parish founded a small missionary church, St Matthew's, on the western fringes of the town, McElheran became its 'director' and, later, as a diocesan lay reader, its 'curate-in-charge.' In 1900, St Matthew's priest assistant was called to be rector of Cronyn Memorial Church back in London, and invited McElheran to come as his lay assistant. By now St Matthew's needed a full-time clergyman, so McElheran, freed from his post as 'curate-in-charge,' accepted the invitation, resigned his newspaper position, returned to London, and worked at the church for two years, supporting himself as a bookkeeper. By 1902 he felt overwhelmed by the call to the ordained ministry, and applied for admission to Wycliffe College.

McElheran was now 25 years old, somewhat short in height and wiry in build, gifted with a fine musical voice, athletic ability, a sense of humour, and a capacity for friendship. He gave the impression of assurance but nervousness too, and he seemed to glow with a warm inner light. The referees who supported his application warned that he was no brilliant student, but they promised that he would work industriously and painstakingly — perhaps, indeed, excessively so, to the point of overtaxing his strength. Above all, they guaranteed that he was earnest in his faith. That faith betrayed a strong strain of other-worldliness; McElheran indicated on his application form that he held himself aloof from frivolous amusements, and he defined a genuine Christian as 'one who keeps himself (through grace) unspotted from the world.' He remained throughout his life a total abstainer, an ardent prohibitionist, and a crusader for rigorous Sunday observance. Principal O'Meara judged that the applicant was 'the stamp of man we want.' He was accepted.

The person with the greatest influence on him was very probably the man he called, with great affection, 'The Chief' — Canon H.J. Cody, rector of St Paul's, Bloor Street, the leading evangelical clergyman in Toronto (before long, in Canada), and the choice of the laity for bishop of Toronto in 1909. McElheran acted as Cody's parish assistant until his graduation in 1907, when Cody flattered him with an offer to be his curate. Equally tempting was an offer from Christ Church Cathedral, Vancouver. But when the wardens of the church nearest his heart, the still humble St Matthew's, Winnipeg, asked the young cleric to replace their departing incumbent, he decided to return there. There he was to stay, in a highly successful ministry, until 1930.

A girl he had met during his first years in Winnipeg, and who had turned up as a parishioner at St Paul's when her family moved to Toronto, returned to Winnipeg at the same time as McElheran. He married her in 1908. Irene Brock came from a respectable Anglican family; her grandfather had helped found Wycliffe College, and her father had founded the Great West Life Assurance Company. She remained active in church affairs all her life, ably chairing various ecclesiastical boards, and travelling widely, especially in the 1930s, campaigning for church restoration funds. They had one son, Brock.

McElheran's ministry at St Matthew's was distinguished by three hallmarks. The first was his evangelical doctrine, which he regarded as 'the pure and simple Gospel.' It centred on the proclamation of Christ's death availing for all, with an individualistic emphasis on personal commitment, self-discipline, and private morality. So powerfully did he preach that one visitor claimed to receive inspiration even from the announcements. So simply and engagingly did he proclaim the Gospel that 'many times,' a student wrote, 'we have watched him talk to an open session of a Sunday School and have seen the children almost transfixed.' If his concern for proper behaviour and attitudes inclined McElheran to be rather rigid, his understanding of redemption convinced him that no sinner was beyond hope; and McElheran's fatherly intercessions saved the jobs of some incautious young people, and even the lives of others convicted of capital offences. He was stern, but he was kindly and loving as well. Second, McElheran was dedicated to missions. For example, as a rector he insisted on directing ten per cent of the church's budget to that purpose; he made his home a virtual way-station for Christian missionaries travelling between eastern Canada and the port of Vancouver; and, when radio was introduced to the public in the second decade of the century, he himself became a kind of electronic missionary, opening his Sunday service to broadcasting. St Matthew's never became a religious club, but always retained a sense of outreach and a drive to evangelize. The third hallmark of McElheran's rectorship was his sense of authority. St Matthew's, his wife later wrote tellingly, 'was *his* church and these people were *his* people.' He could not shepherd his flock effectively without the exercise of strong personal authority. In this respect, indeed, McElheran was not uncharacteristic of other Anglican clergy of the age. Once a year, at a church meeting, McElheran offered his resignation, and withdrew from the room while his parishioners decided (as they always did) to recommit themselves to his charge;

for the next twelve months the people's duty was to obey their rector. Unwilling, or conscientiously unable, to delegate authority, he overworked, but his ministry was exciting. By 1930 that little missionary church he had begun in 1898 had grown into reportedly the largest and wealthiest church in the Canadian North West, with the largest Sunday school in all of Canada. He became in succession rural dean, a canon, and an archdeacon. He served the national church faithfully as well, on various councils and commissions. For Wycliffe in 1916 he carried on some delicate negotiations with the primate, the archbishop of Rupert's Land, during the controversy over the Wycliffe College Act of 1916, which removed control over Wycliffe's theological degrees from the episcopacy. Wycliffe used its degree-granting powers under this Act at its golden jubilee convocation in 1927 to bestow an honorary doctorate on McElheran himself.

In 1930, when Principal O'Meara died, the trustees of Wycliffe invited McElheran to take over the principalship. It is significant that they preferred the administrative head of the college to be a pastor (as O'Meara himself had been) rather than an academic. McElheran had, it appears, quietly declined nominations to two bishoprics in order to carry on his work in Winnipeg among the people he loved; but after much prayer he was led to believe that this new offer was a call from God. He wrapped up affairs at St Matthew's, took a month's holiday, and moved into the principal's residence with his wife, their son, and the family's fox terrier in the summer of 1930. The costs of the transition almost ruined him financially, as we know from his personal correspondence in the college archives, but there is not the least indication that he ever complained publicly, unless one thinks of his early acknowledgment that the adjustment from western parish to urban academy had 'bristled with difficulties.'

The new principal took up his duties at Wycliffe when it was the largest theological college in Canada of a religious tradition to which he personally was totally committed, a theological conscience of the church. He keenly felt the obligation of loyalty to the alma mater whose son he was, of conformity to the ideals of an institution which had been moulded by other hands. 'It is not mine to do as I like,' he explained to the trustees at the end of his first academic year in 1931, and time and again thereafter he would say 'the College's direction has been determined by its Founders.' Canada, indeed, had changed since 1877, and so had the church; it was a new day with new challenges; but the college would succeed, McElheran believed, not by modifications in its purpose or by major institutional changes, but by the reaffirmation of its traditional principles.

Such changes as McElheran set out to make can be briefly summarized. First, he stabilized the college's finances, which were dangerously tied to shaky investments, more by cutting costs than by trying to wring money from the church in the midst of the Depression. Second, he tightened academic standards. For instance, the college became more selective in its admissions. Fewer students were needed, because fewer new clergy were being ordained during this period of retrenchment. McElheran picked with care the applicants whose papers would reach the Committee on Students to be considered for admission. The number with B.A.s or M.A.s in the graduating class jumped from three out of sixteen in 1931 to eight out of eight in 1939. He sought to encourage academic excellence in another way by asking fifty friends of the College to endow new prizes for good work. Third, McElheran introduced into the curriculum an honours programme, a lecture series in church architecture, church music, and first aid, examinations of students' familiarity with the English Bible, and a course called 'The Principal's Hour.' The names, contents, and relations of some existing academic courses were shuffled about somewhat. Finally, McElheran set out to improve students' elocution. 'I feel that if a man is not a good reader,' he said, 'he really has very little justification for remaining in the ministry at all.' Applicants with major speech impediments were not admitted; students with minor impediments were sent to the dentist or provided with special training. McElheran could not stomach such pronunciations as 'noo' for 'new,' '-in'' for '-ing,' 'jennilmin' for 'gentlemen,' 'Trawna' for 'Toronto.' He made a list of the most grievous mispronunciations, arranged them in a sentence, and required entering students to appear alone before him and read it over and over until they got it right. The sentence was: 'Toronto is a new city worth talking about; it has beautiful walks beside the water, towards which gentlemen have the kindliest feelings.'

McElheran's style of leadership at Wycliffe resembled his style at St Matthew's; he was not merely the administrative head of the college, but, as it were, the pastor of a parish. At the college as in the parish, he proclaimed doctrine, supported missions, and exercised strong authority.

In doctrine, the new principal was an evangelical. But his love for the church led him to adopt in public a gentlemanly and tolerant posture towards non-evangelicals, and under his principalship Wycliffe shared with neighbouring Trinity College some public lectures, some alumni meetings, and even a convocation. But his friends well knew his strong personal conviction that, as he put it, 'not compromise but championship is our strength.' He regarded Anglo-Catholicism as a road to unbelief, because, as he most firmly pronounced, it was not based on the Gospel. The experience of some parts of the Church of England, he thought, proved his case: it had abandoned the New Testament for sacerdotalism and medievalism, and it had lost its congregations. Hence the importance of the college's duty to protect students, and sometimes faculty members too, and the whole church, from Anglo-Catholic error. The danger, the principal said on one occasion, was even greater than it had been in 1877; again, after an Anglo-Catholic mission in Massey Hall, he warned, 'These people, who used to be so cautious, ... are now pressing forward in the most audacious way.'

The rivalry, indeed the bitterness, between Anglo-Catholic and evangelical is rather startling to our own generation, which can much more easily endorse the prophetic words of the principal's colleague, Professor Pilcher, about a hypothetical Christian: 'He is a sincere disciple of the Lord Jesus Christ; and that is of infinitely more importance than his being an evangelical or an Anglo-Catholic.' But to many at the time the difference seemed far more radical than that statement admitted. To some evangelicals the choice was between Gospel and unbelief; to some Anglo-Catholics, between loyalty to the church and total subjectivism. We begin to see now that much of the difference was really one of metaphysics. The Anglo-Catholics supposed that the Gospel was best understood in the thought categories of the Greek and Latin Fathers, while the evangelicals preferred the expressions and emphases of the English and German Reformers. The Barthians, meanwhile, were seeing Scripture less as something ripe for metaphysical formulation than as the history of the dialogue between God and man, God speaking, man responding. Students of this 'dialectical theology' were prepared to see a continuing unfolding of God's purpose in the world, unanticipated by formulas wrought in the doctrinal disputes of the past. For McElheran, however, truth was not historical but eternal, not to be sought in the contemporary and immediate situation, but to be imported from a realm that transcended history. God's purpose was to be found revealed not so much *in* the world as *outside* it and *in spite of* it. McElheran urged Wycliffe's alumni in 1933 to be 'the custodians of a definite tradition and the upholders of definite principles which remain the same in spite of changed conditions.'

A second characteristic of McElheran's principalship was his continuing concern with Christian missions. He revitalized a spirit that had informed the college from its inception and had inspired the whole Canadian church for two generations. In his first official report to the college council, the principal announced his desire to spark a 'revival of interest in the missionary motive.' Honorary degrees were given to missionaries and officials of missionary societies, a programme for medical missionaries was begun, old-time missionary meetings were featured at alumni meetings, numerous parish missions were sponsored by the college (as we shall observe again presently), an issue of the student literary magazine, *Cap and Gown*, was devoted to missions at the principal's express request, an all-night urban mission at 260 Parliament Street was manned by Wycliffe students; students were encouraged to take up missionary positions, especially after 1937 when such opportunities increased; a 'Fellowship of Evangelism' and missionary prayer groups met at the college, a cycle of prayer for Canadian missionaries was produced, two week-long schools of Evangelism were held for ministers; and in 1937 there was even a recommendation from the alumni to reinstate the Wycliffe missions, which had long since been integrated into the Canadian Church Mission Society.

Again, like the rector of St Matthew's, the principal of Wycliffe exercised a full personal authority over his charge. 'The Principal is responsible,' McElheran read in a statement of policy to his very first meeting with the faculty, 'for seeing that the general trend and tendency is always consistent with the principles of the College as they have been maintained through the years ... [T]here must be only one head to the College.' With this philosophy at its foundation, the college leadership was characterized above all by a strong sense of authority, a certain paternalism, and loyalty to tradition.

The principal's sense of authority bordered on what some might call nowadays 'defensiveness.' He wanted to limit the men's time in residence, since senior men, he felt, adopted 'an air of proprietorship' and wanted to 'control' the institution. He considered at one point scrapping the *Cap and Gown* because it was 'controlled by students' and 'did the College no good.' When the magazine was strapped for funds, McElheran conditioned the college's financial support on a greater student 'cooperation' with him. Although the principal experimented democratically with allowing graduating students to elect the recipient of the prize for general proficiency, he quickly terminated the plan when it 'failed to produce the desired results.' When in 1934 the students autonomously invited a German rabbi to describe Nazi oppression, an appalled McElheran immediately pressed through the Executive Committee of the college a resolution prohibiting any addresses in the college without the principal's permission.

But, if the principal sometimes tended towards the authoritarian, it was not because he loved power but because he wanted to do what was best for his students. He helped them set up a most lively form of parliamentary student government. He gave a real impetus to the athletic programme. He arranged generous financial aid for students, and frequently found college funds to cover their medical expenses and other debts, though sometimes he worried (paternalistically) that if he made things *too* easy he would be taken for granted. During one examination period it occurred to him to arrange cocoa and biscuits for a study break at 10 P.M. every night. He found jobs for all graduates, arranging interim financial assistance when necessary. He assigned summer missions and Sunday parish duties to his students, personally negotiating the terms, without, however, consulting the students themselves. It is not hard to see how McElheran might have exasperated the students, but in the final analysis he leaves the impression that he loved them almost as he did his own family.

McElheran once described the goal of the college as producing 'men who will be loyal to the Church, to the Prayer Book, and to the Bible.' The term 'loyalty' sprang readily to McElheran's lips, and it represents in a word the ambience of Wycliffe College in the 1940s. 'Loyalty' may seem to some modern sensibilities a trifle anaemic, a secondary ethic at best, but to McElheran it connoted a sacrifice of private advantage in furtherance of a cause of transcendent value, and a personal sharing in its glory. His purpose as principal was to socialize Anglican postulants for Orders into the ideal of loyal daily obedience to duty. One graduate recalls a spring day when McElheran peremptorily ordered him to take a summer charge in Saskatchewan shortly after exams, and he recalls also a day that summer when a postcard arrived from McElheran: 'What you are doing day after day is the greatest work in the world.' Loyalty demanded discipline and sacrifice, but it issued in fulfilment and peace. No one illustrated loyalty more nobly than the principal himself, in his industry in every department of the life of the church, in his defence of the prayer book's conceptions of prayer and praise and worship, in his devotion to the principles of scriptural evangelicalism in which he had been nurtured, in his unfailing commitment to the welfare of his students, as he perceived it. But to be totally loyal to a tradition, as McElheran strived to be, was to defend all of it, to leave nothing behind. To question, to re-evaluate, to criticize, even to analyse, raised the suspicion of moral weakness. Faith tried to meet new challenges — the Depression crisis in values and ideals, modern biblical scholarship, new visions of the relation of

God to the world, social and political reconstruction — by denying their ultimate importance and returning instead to the familiar formulas and disputes of a particular tradition.

The faculty, however, was diversified in outlook, and indeed tensions involving the college tradition in the narrow sense often appear just beneath the surface. Of this faculty Canon Cody once said, 'In my judgment there is no finer theological group in Canada.' During this decade there was nearly a complete turnover in the personnel of the faculty, but its academic quality remained consistently high and its representation of the evangelical spectrum remained wide.

William Edington Taylor (1877-1967) was born in London and came to Canada to be educated as a missionary. He took his B.A. with a first class in philosophy, and his record at Wycliffe was outstanding, except for homiletics and elocution, in which he was only very good. He took his M.A. and his Ph.D. from the University of Toronto, simultaneously lecturing part-time at Wycliffe. He served as a missionary at Hankow and Shanghai from 1906 to 1918. He was appointed to the Wycliffe staff in 1923 in apologetics, but the name of the department was changed, at his request, to 'history and philosophy of religion' under McElheran. Taylor apparently undertook relatively little original scholarly research. His only published work of note in that line concerned Bishop Butler, the eighteenth-century Anglican apologist. Taylor argued that Butler had tried, 'not to prove the divine existence,' which had already been admitted by his contemporary opponents, but 'to show that the God of nature ... is a God known' through historical revelation as well. Seen in this light, Taylor concluded, Butler's arguments 'were eminently satisfactory' and retained apologetic value even in the twentieth century. Throughout his teaching career he sought to understand, and to criticize philosophically, movements which repudiated or neglected faith in God. He perceived that much of the modern world, like Butler's England, was departing from traditional Christian views.

Taylor was mild-mannered (one student said a 'jolly' fellow), less severe than McElheran, and had enjoyed a long experience with students, not only as a teacher but also in youth organizations. Students of the time recall that in the periods when he was acting principal — in 1928-30 before McElheran's arrival, and in 1939-40, after his death — the college ran smoothly. There is no evidence why the trustees passed him by in choosing a principal in 1929, but it was perhaps because they wanted another practical parish priest, as O'Meara had been.

Dyson Hague (1857-1935), an 1882 graduate of Wycliffe and its professor of liturgics (while also rector of the Church of the Messiah), was of all the staff the most uncompromising 'low-Church' partisan. He was an indefatigable controversialist and a prolific writer with a peculiar stylistic habit of marking those of his statements that carried divine authority by couching them in King James's English. Hague firmly believed that to question the historicity of a single story of prophecy or divine intervention in the Bible was to repudiate the authority of the whole. Moreover, Hague was virtually a fundamentalist about the prayer book, which, he maintained, had been composed and corrected by convinced evangelical reformers guided by God's spirit. 'The Church *was* reformed. The Church *is* reformed. It ought not to be reformed again. We must not change the character of the Church of England.'

But there was another side to Hague. He read the liturgy with beauty and drama, and preached with power and clarity. His conviction in controversy won him the respect of his opponents, and his strength of character won him the affection of his students. His self-assurance, which some thought egotism, excited the awe of everyone. Dyson Hague stories and legends abounded. There was the apocryphal story, for example, that Hague once warned General Synod that only three people in Canada were competent to edit the new hymn book. Asked to name them, he is supposed to have answered, 'Well, myself for one, and — I've forgotten the names of the other two.'

Benjamin William Horan (1893-1953), professor at various times of New Testament, Old Testament, and patristics, and dean of residence, took his B.A. in 1916 at Trinity College, Dublin, with a first class testimonium which placed him at about the top five per cent of his class, and proceeded to the B.D. there in 1919. He began teaching at Wycliffe in 1922, and married the sister of Canon Cody's future second wife. Although he resigned in 1933 to take up the vice-principalship of London College of Divinity, England (also called St John's, Highbury), he asked McElheran the following year to be allowed to return to Wycliffe, apparently because administration did not suit him. The College Council acceded, but with some reluctance, since members felt that 'this kind of reinstatement was seldom satisfactory.' He enjoyed a marvellous facility in Greek and Latin. He kept himself informed of new developments in scholarship, which related the New Testament to the history of the early church communities that had produced it and demonstrated a development in scriptural views of the nature of Christ. Scripture he took not as a rule-book but as a record of the history of salvation; doctrines were the 'crystallizations' of spiritual experience.

Articles Horan published later reflect his struggles with the received evangelical orthodoxy. The older evangelicals, he wrote, had been 'unaware of the meaning of the changes that were taking place, and unable or unwilling to meet them.' He regarded Scripture not as revelation but as the container of revelation, like 'the casket with the jewel inside'; the Resurrection he took as 'a sublime, cosmic event'; the ways of God with humankind he found not predictable but 'sometimes difficult to understand.' Curiously, he once attributed the Epistle to the Hebrews to Priscilla; after finding other supports for the speculation, he added, 'I like to think that God has employed at least one woman in the formation of the New Testament.'

Thomas William Isherwood (1899-1957) taught systematic theology, and later, early church history, from 1926. He took his B.A. at Brasenose College, Oxford, and his theology diploma at Wycliffe Hall, Oxford, in 1921. He married a graduate of the Deaconess Institute connected with Wycliffe in 1931. He read Barth's work carefully, interpreting it for his students and popularizing it for Canadian lay people. His students remember him for his clear and interesting lectures, his ready humour, and his personal interest in them. He preached powerfully and built up a reputation as a parish missioner; perhaps at heart he remained a parish priest. He left Wycliffe in 1938 to return to England as vicar of Christ Church, Claughton, Birkenhead. He later returned to Canada, first as director of the Canadian School of Missions, and then as rector of St Paul's Church, Halifax.

Charles Venn Pilcher (1879-1961) was the great-great-great-grandson of Henry Venn, the English evangelical leader of the eighteenth century. His father, a native Australian, was rector of St Clement's, Oxford, and his mother one of its Sunday school superintendents. One of his brothers was a priest, another a missionary in Ceylon. He attended Hertford College, Oxford, where he took his B.A. (1902), B.D. (1909), and D.D. (1921). His early hopes of missionary activity were dashed by poor health, and at Principal O'Meara's invitation he came to Canada and lectured at Wycliffe from 1906 to 1908. He then served Toronto parishes until 1919, when he was made professor of Old Testament at Wycliffe. When Horan left temporarily in 1933, he took over New Testament; Horan, on his return, then replaced Pilcher in Old Testament. Pilcher also taught church history briefly, and lectured in homiletics and church music. His lecture style was highly imaginative; in fact, it was at his behest that the college bought its first magic lantern, as a visual aid for his classes.

Though personally an evangelical, Pilcher far transcended divisions of churchmanship in his influence and came to be one of the most highly regarded clergymen in Canada. He valued highly the 'social righteousness' of evangelical leaders of the eighteenth and early nineteenth centuries — and, as he pointed out, of John Wycliffe himself. A courageous social pioneer in Canada, he pressed vigorously for disarmament, prison reform, economic justice, community welfare services, and other liberal causes. He was president of the Social Service Council of Canada, a progressive and influential interdenominational agency.

He was also an accomplished musician. He played bass clarinet in the Toronto Symphony Orchestra until he was expelled by the union, which refused to let him play without fee. He composed hymns (including the Wycliffe hymn, 'King of Love, O Christ, We Crown Thee'). He fought for the improvement of church music in periodical articles, through summer courses with composer Healey Willan and baritone J. Campbell McInnes, and as the first and thus far only canon precentor of the diocese of Toronto.

He was, too, a liturgical critic. He wrote in a 1932 issue of the *Canadian Churchman*, 'The tone of the Prayer Book is "quietist," not challenging; it is sedative, not rousing ... In the "Prayer for All Sorts and Conditions of Men" we hand the burden of the needy over to God. There is no suggestion that we should ourselves do anything about it!' The implication, typical of him, was that social concerns should be joined with worship.

Graduates remember Pilcher's kindliness and gentleness, his graciousness and charm of manner, his love of poetry and beauty, the warmth of his relations with students. He left Wycliffe in 1936 to become bishop coadjutor of Sydney, after having been assured that he would be allowed to teach at a theological college there.

Aside from a number of sessional appointments in miscellaneous fields like Greek, reading and public speaking, pedagogy, and canon law — they included, for example, Ramsay Armitage and Leslie Hunt, his two immediate successors as principal — McElheran recommended two major faculty appointments, one in New Testament and one in systematic theology. A graduate later wrote to Armitage, 'If Principal McElheran had done nothing else — and he did much — we would be under great debt to him both in the College and in the Canadian Church for his appointments of F.D. Coggan from Cambridge and F.W. Dillistone from Oxford.'

Frederick Donald Coggan (1909-), a curate in Islington and lecturer at Manchester University, had taken his B.A. from St John's College, Cambridge, in 1931, and his theology diploma from Wycliffe Hall, Oxford, in 1934. When he met Coggan in London while visiting England looking for a professor of New Testament, McElheran was impressed with the young man and gave him the job. Coggan arrived at Wycliffe in 1937 and quickly earned the respect of his students and the confidence of his faculty colleagues. He was genial, enthusiastic about things Canadian, gifted as an organist and choirmaster, natural and clear in his public addresses, impressive as a radio evangelist, learned in his scholarship.

Soon after joining the Wycliffe faculty, Coggan became dean of residence. He quickly became active in all aspects of collegiate life, devoting himself also to preaching engagements across Canada. His first book, in 1944, was significantly the *Canadian Lenten Book*, an annual publication of the church, in which he issued an appeal for greater and deeper reading of the Bible, as he esteemed it, 'a people's heritage.' In 1941 he took a General Synod B.D. through Wycliffe and in 1944 received the honorary degree of Doctor of Divinity from Wycliffe in recognition of the ministry he had exercised not only in the college but in the Canadian church as a whole.

Appointed principal of the London College of Divinity, Coggan left Wycliffe in 1944 for the new post he was to hold until 1955 when he became bishop of Bradford. This honour was later followed by elevation to the archbishopric of York, and in 1974 he became archbishop of Canterbury and primate of all England.

Less need be said in this chapter about Frederick William Dillistone (1903-00), since he arrived at Wycliffe in 1938, only a few months before McElheran's final incapacity. An outstanding theologian, he had majored in 'mathematical moderations' at Brasenose College, Oxford, and received his B.D. in 1924 from Wycliffe Hall, Oxford, where he also tutored. He had served the church as a missionary and as a parish priest. A graduate recalls with appreciation that by both his teaching style and his examinations he challenged his students to think creatively and theologically.

Professor Dillistone began at Wycliffe a writing ministry that was to earn him a world-wide reputation as one of the major Anglican theologians of his time. His primary ministry, however, continued to be by the spoken word in classroom and pulpit. In the latter he excelled and held a succession of distinguished appointments as vice-president of the London College of Divinity, professor at the Episcopal Theological School, Cambridge, Massachusetts, dean of Liverpool Cathedral, and fellow of Oriel College, Oxford.

Two other staff members deserve mention. Richard Mercer-Wilson (1887-00) left the college a year after McElheran's arrival to become general secretary of the Religious Tract Society. The two may possibly have suffered from a personality difference. John Nelson Blodgett (1876-1939), a Wycliffe graduate and former missionary and parish priest, served his alma mater steadfastly from 1925 until his death as field secretary and financial secretary. 'Prester John,' as he was nicknamed, raised donations, recruited candidates for the ministry, found summer mission placements for students, and sometimes advised them on study habits. McElheran himself acted as professor of practical theology and homiletics.

At this time students were kept at a distance from the faculty; they learned to regard professors, as one student recalls, as 'a higher order of being.' Another remembers that a summons to the principal's office caused shivers, and the termination of the interview brought a sigh of relief. Students would scarcely dream of sharing intimate problems or theological doubts with most staff members, for fear of discipline or shame.

Students had to meet several tests before they could be admitted to, or allowed to continue in, the diploma programme. First, they had to be men. The programme was intended to prepare people for the priesthood, and women could not be priests — the Lambeth Conference of 1930 had reaffirmed that. The single exception to this rule in the decade was one Mabel Jones, who, being single, could at least be admitted to deacon's Orders. She entered the college under O'Meara's principalship and in 1931 became Wycliffe's first female graduate. But her picture did not appear in the group photograph of graduating students, and the principal, in listing the year's diplomates in his report to the council, left her name out of the typescript and had to scribble it in the margin at the last moment. Jones afterwards served as a teacher and missionary among the Indians of the North until 1950. In 1937, a married woman, Nancy Smith (Mrs Reginald Goldwin Smith), completed all the college's academic requirements with distinguished standing; she was nevertheless denied the diploma because she was a woman and so ineligible for Orders. (She finally received the diploma from Principal Armitage in 1953.) The men were, however, exposed to the existence of women in some of their university courses, and students at the Deaconess Institute and a handful of other women were permitted to take certain divinity courses with the men.

Second, a prospective Wycliffe student had to be young. It was rare for a man over 25 to be admitted to the basic course.

Third, the candidate had to be single. Even an engagement was a matter for suspicion. Very occasionally a student married secretly. Inevitably the news reached the principal and, when it did, the student was expelled by the Committee on Students. By the end of the 1930s these old celibate ideals were already on the wane, and the threatened college officials responded by redoubling their vigilance. Prospective students were now explicitly asked on their application forms, 'Are you married or engaged to be married?'

Fourth, a Wycliffe student had to be healthy. Applicants for admission were required to submit satisfactory medical reports. For example, a student with a history of occasional epileptic fits was turned down without further consideration. Speech impediments were the most common medical reason for refusal. The dangers of allowing unhealthy students into the college were demonstrated by one young man who entered in apparently good health but developed a polinoidal cyst in his back which his physician certified, 'I have no doubt troubles him considerably.' The discomfort, and the inevitable anxiety about an operation, prevented the student from falling asleep at night, and he frequently overslept in the morning. He did poorly in his course work, and eventually left the college. After several operations he was readmitted under Principal Armitage, completed his theology, and was ordained.

Fifth, a Wycliffe student had to be an Anglican. In many ways, it is true, the 1930s were an ecumenical age. The principal himself attended the Faith and Order Conference in Edinburgh in 1937, an important forerunner of the World Council of Churches; there was talk of union with the United Church; many Anglicans deplored the wasteful competition and extravagant duplication of effort of Protestant churches in the mission field and, indeed, at home. But it seemed vital, nevertheless, to preserve Wycliffe as a wholly Anglican college, and applicants from other traditions were required to receive episcopal confirmation. On one occasion a professor had to rush an ex-Presbyterian through a crash catechetical course before presentation to the bishop.

Sixth, the student's sympathies had to be evangelical. The principal took it upon himself to turn away heterodox enquirers, and the Committee on Students expected evidence in each application of an evangelical call to ministry. McElheran introduced forms with such questions as, 'Are you sincerely in sympathy with our principles?' 'Do you expect that (as an alumnus you will be) able to give happy and loyal service in accordance with our traditions and position?' All students were required to answer each question and attach their signature. 'If there are men in this College who are not loyal,' McElheran told the faculty at his first meeting with them, 'or who will not bring their voice and conduct into harmony with the prevailing spirit of the Institution, I shall immediately and without consultation dismiss such students, and I shall do it without the right of appeal. This I intend to make very plain to the men at the beginning.'

Finally, the college demanded of its students defined standards of behaviour. McElheran expected his men to respond to God's grace with sincere efforts at personal righteousness. In the summer of 1936, a Wycliffe student had a beer at a parish young people's picnic with the church organist and, a little later, in the course of a discussion, momentarily lost his temper and apparently said something to hurt the organist's feelings. The organist retaliated by informing the college authorities of the episode. Horan was sent to the parish to interview the organist and file a report. He asked the organist

if B—— could be said to be drunk and the reply was 'far from it.' I asked if he had ever seen B—— under the influence of drink on any other occasion and he replied 'no.' I asked if any other members of the party remarked on B——'s behaviour and I was told 'no.' I asked if he had ever observed B—— doing or saying anything that deserved censure and he replied 'no.'

Horan's general impression was that the organist was biased and hypocritical, but the Committee on Students viewed the scandal very gravely, and expelled the student without giving reasons. On another occasion, a report reached the college authorities that a certain student was simultaneously engaged to two girls. The rumour proved false but, just to be on the safe side, McElheran put the student on strict probation.

The rigours of college officialdom inevitably provoked from students some rebellious horseplay — unauthorized fire drills, ribaldry from the gallery during a stuffy convocation, and so on. (The recollections of graduates in this area seem uncommonly vivid!)

Most of the men who met all the college's standards were admitted to residence directly from high school. They then studied Arts next door at University College in the University of Toronto in preparation for the theology instruction given in Wycliffe itself. The college diploma was not a degree. Graduates of the regular course waited a year and then wrote a series of ten college examinations for the certificate of the Licentiate in Theology (L.Th.). After 1931, however, an honours course was established (on the principal's recommendation) in addition to the regular course; graduates from the honours course received the L.Th. without further examination. The B.D. and the 'in course' D.D. were graduate degrees, examined by a committee of General Synod.

The curriculum itself seemed on paper to be well defined, even inflexible, but deviations from the norm were frequent. Besides the 'regular' seven-year programme which included the B.A., there were 'special' six-year and five-year programmes. Some students took courses out of sequence in order to equalize class sizes from year to year. Students were permitted certain theology courses as part of their Arts programmes (these were called 'Religious Knowledge Options'): the faculty had discovered that young students subject to an unrelieved barrage of university secularism often became demoralized. A special problem here, however, was that the examination schedules of the university differed from those of the college, and conflicts occurred in some cases. Some students successfully petitioned exemptions from certain courses. Some might be required to attend the lectures but be exempted from the examinations. Many students had to repeat courses because of previous failures. Failures were extremely common, perhaps because every student was taking ten or fifteen courses, most of which were evaluated by an examination given during a short period at the end of term. True, it was common for the faculty to raise the better failures to passes before the marks went on record, and in the event students had a second chance with supplementary examinations. Even so, in 1939, the *best* year of the decade in this respect, the principal proudly reported that of twenty-nine students only eight had failed one or more examinations.

The frequency of all these special cases produced disorder, and often a student might discover too late that he had taken the wrong course, or neglected to take the right course, or missed an examination, or made some other such mistake. The faculty frequently had to discuss whether to give retroactive approval to him to make other arrangements for these situations, and from time to time it discussed ways and means of keeping abreast of where each student was in his programme.

In principle, the residence was the community of men studying for Orders at Wycliffe. There were two general exceptions. First, senior theology students with parishes and students whose parents' homes were in Toronto were generally granted permission to live out of residence. Second, beginning in 1934, a few carefully selected non-theologues were allowed to live in the college. The decision, which ultimately transformed the character of residence life, was taken because new admissions to divinity were too few to fill the places of graduates, and the residence would lose too much revenue without non-theological boarders. Room and board was $5 per week. Bursary assistance generally ran from $120 to $300 per student; graduates who spent less than seven years' service in the church after graduation were expected to return the money. Residents wore gowns, did not entertain ladies, and (to state the rule broadly) did not stay out past 11:30 P.M. They did not dance, and when an editor of *Cap and Gown* merely *mentioned* a dance in print, a staff member scolded him, 'You'll never know what harm you've done.' The social highlight of the year was the 'At-Home,' a genteel affair which before 1935 featured a musical recital and light refreshments, but which beginning in 1935 included a college dinner.

Meals in the refectory cost 25 cents each. Acting Principal Taylor and Principal McElheran made dietary quality a priority, with considerable success. Health remained a problem throughout the decade, however. Influenza and infections, especially nose and throat infections, were common. Between 1930 and 1933, for example, ten students required tonsillectomies. The year 1935 was especially bad for influenza and operations, and one student died. The college began requiring annual medical examinations for students. The occasional report of a duodenal ulcer or a nervous breakdown suggests that a contributory factor in the high incidence of disease may have been the pressures of college life in these days — intensive periods of academic examination, rigorous moral regulation, and the enforcement of theological orthodoxy.

Regular presence at chapel was required, although scarcely a year went by that some official record or another did not include an expression of someone's concern at the students' poor chapel attendance. Formal head counts ceased in 1933, being recognized by then as an exercise in futility, but insufficient devotion did not go unnoticed. Morning prayer occupied twenty to thirty minutes before breakfast at 8:10, with faculty members officiating, and, naturally, the prayer book service. Evening prayer followed the 6 P.M. dinner in the early part of the decade, preceded it in the later. In addition, there were frequent devotional periods and prayer meetings.

First-year students sat in the front pews, and many remember how from that vantage point they felt greatly overawed by the officiating faculty, especially McElheran in the pulpit. Other students were assigned pews further back in proportion to their seniority, with faculty in the back stalls from which they could observe their charges.

The training of young men for the ministry by no means exhausted the college's interests. It would be more correct to say that theological education constituted only a means to an end. The college's real purpose was to strengthen Canadian Anglicanism, safeguard evangelical principles against Anglo-Catholicism, and help lead the Gospel of Christ to victory in the world. The college leadership perceived the church militant as an army struggling to save human souls, and the job of Wycliffe was not only to train recruits and send out loyal Christian soldiers marching as to war, but also to bolster allied morale, secure loyalty, support the parish outposts with men and material, and advise headquarters in matters of policy.

A first priority for McElheran was to re-open communications between Wycliffe and 'Wycliffe parishes,' that is, congregations where graduates had charge. He set out to visit his alumni in the Maritimes during his first summer after arriving in Toronto. The trip had its discouraging moments. Many Maritime areas had Anglo-Catholic traditions, and some former Wycliffites had yielded to them. Some men, he discovered, retained unhappy memories of college life and still harboured resentment, a few having actually finished their work at High-Church King's College, Halifax. The curate at one of the most important Wycliffe parishes — St Paul's, Halifax, whose rectors had included Hague and the senior Armitage — said he had petitioned several times for permission to complete his theology at Wycliffe extramurally, and had never received an answer; he was continuing studies at King's. (He later made the appropriate arrangements with McElheran.) McElheran succeeded in warming up many of these relations, and he affirmed to the College Council that these visits were a necessity, regardless of the college's financial situation. In fact, he or a faculty colleague undertook the demanding work of visiting graduates in some part of the country or another during every summer afterwards. McElheran also kept communication open with graduates by mail. In December 1932 a college mailing rallied loyalties with an enthusiastic pep talk. 'Materially the days are dark and the times are difficult,' it admitted, but 'spiritually the outlook is brighter and days of difficulty are always days of challenge!' The principal encouraged graduates with problems to write to him, and he described his office as 'a sort of perpetual clinic' on graduates' affairs. Similarly, at the alumni executive's request, he sought to ensure the evangelical loyalties of college men by lending them selected edifying books by mail from the college library.

The college's generally welcome efforts to boost the morale and support the evangelical loyalties of its alumni in the parish did little to help graduates meet the real problems facing them in the 1930s — poverty, unemployment, starvation, cold, despair, ineffective government. McElheran visited a parish in northern Saskatchewan which contained 2,600 people on relief, and not a single church building; the principal feared that the priest, a graduate, would be 'crippled by the strain of the work.' When he went to visit another graduate there, he found him in a mental hospital. Professor Isherwood found in Saskatchewan drought-stricken farms with homes made of logs and mud plaster, and 'a stream of pathetic caravans' wearily driving emaciated cattle along rutted dirt roads. 'The Christian Church has proved herself able to do little or nothing' for such people, he confessed. Nor had the college done much to equip its students specifically for these conditions. A recent graduate exhausted by overwork wrote sarcastically in *Cap and Gown*, ' "The Church Invisible" makes a splendid theme for the lecture in the classroom, but it is the Church Visible through which the common preachers have to get things done.' Other writers in *Cap and Gown*, especially early in the decade, downplayed the ritualistic and denominational divisions of the church and hinted at the need for training leading to a more realistic understanding of society. Some looked for a theology which would relate Christian faith to the new political and economic situation: for example, one said, to the inward spiritual ideals of the labour movement.

Many evangelicals, however, including McElheran, believed that the ills of society stemmed from personal sinfulness; the principal helped draft a statement approved by the Toronto Synod in 1937 which blamed the economic situation on 'the unfaithfulness of some Christians.' Ministers were needed, not to deal with social symptoms, but to attack the disease of unbelief. McElheran's heart went out to individual sufferers, and he was personally active in charitable and welfare organizations, especially the Federation for Community Service. But proposals to restructure society disturbed him because they seemed to distract attention from the real issue. Communism, especially, threatened him deeply. He saw society as a battlefield between Communism and Christianity, and prophesied in 1934 that one of the two would certainly be vanquished by the other in twenty-five years. He worried which would be the victor. Communists, he said, were a hundred times more devoted to their cause than most Christians to theirs. At all hours of the day, one could hear Communism advocated by students in Hart House, the student union, and even, he hinted darkly, by professors in their classrooms. The college's way of training students for the Depression church, in short, was to re-invigorate the proclamation of evangelical principles, and expose Communist hopes as chimerical. Salvation was more important than milk supplies, as one speaker bluntly told the college's diamond jubilee alumni meetings in 1937.

The college therefore led the Anglican church in a new evangelization. Faculty members preached and addressed church groups, McElheran himself the most regularly and vigorously of all. Evangelical tracts, pamphlets, and articles in the *Canadian Churchman* and other periodicals were published. The college also sponsored numerous missions and missionary meetings in parish churches. These meetings were much tamer than American-style revivalism. They amounted to talks and services in the 'free-church' style intended to attract and convert non-believers and lukewarm churchgoers. Frequently they ended with an invitation to the laity to commit themselves to Christ; mission cards might be distributed with a statement such as, 'I accept Christ as my Saviour and in his strength dedicate my life to His service,' with one portion for the signator and one to leave with the rector. Parish missions led by missioners invited by the college both from inside Canada and from abroad were numerous throughout the decade, especially after 1934. McElheran and the College Council were in fact prepared to appoint a full-time college missioner if a suitable candidate could be found. In this enterprise the college sought simply to discharge its responsibilities to the church; it frequently suffered a financial loss — in spite of free-will money offerings, which the church wardens sometimes unilaterally sequestered for the parish.

In 1935 McElheran announced plans for an 'Evangel Mission Movement' to spark a new Canadian revival. The most significant result was a series of missions in May and June 1936, featuring the Reverend Bryan Green, who was then still a young English vicar, an Oxford University chaplain, and a member of the archbishop of Canterbury's Committee on Evangelism. A series of evening missions with Green at St Paul's, Bloor Street, was announced with posters and brochures featuring a statement by an English bishop to the effect that

> the greatest and most pressing need of the time is a spiritual revival in the Church. The appalling indifference to the things of God and the soul which prevails among all sections of society, the insolence and aggressiveness of evil on our streets and in all forms of literature, the decay of home religion and decline in public worship, together with the increase of secularism and infidelity in our midst [make penitence and prayer necessary].

The statement reflects the sense of urgency, the suspicion of certain currents in contemporary culture and society, the relative indifference to merely material concerns, and the appeal to individualism and personal morality which also characterized McElheran's attitudes. The principal clearly reflected the feelings of large numbers of Anglicans, who were very probably comforted and inspired by the college's evangelization. The same refrain was sounded in an invitation to young women from 18 to 35 to hear Green use Christianity to fill the void left by the disappearance of 'old standards and conventions,' including those governing 'the sex instinct.' Finally, Green taught a school of evangelism at the college to interested ministers who might then carry the mission technique to churches in their own areas.

Defeating Anglo-Catholicism within the church and Communism without required a more devoutly evangelical institutional church, the college believed, and Wycliffe men championed their cause in ecclesiastical courts and through *ad hoc* pressure groups. The role of lay friends of the college seemed promising. In 1935, an evangelical Laymen's Association was appointed by the council. A trustee was chairman, but many expected that McElheran would informally direct its activity, as he himself only discovered later. Representatives were invited from a number of evangelical parishes. The minutes, interestingly, indicate that the laymen explicitly recognized that their views were falling out of favour with younger Anglicans. The most immediate issue, however, was that Anglo-Catholic forces were calling for a revision of the Canadian Prayer Book (which was substantially the 1662 English Prayer Book), and the Cowley Fathers were publishing pamphlets urging changes which evangelicals regarded as pre-Reformation or Roman Catholic in character. The Laymen's Association hoped to marshal letters, petitions, propaganda campaigns, and discussion groups, but when McElheran himself, weighted down with a myriad other obligations, failed to supply sufficient personal leadership, the group faltered. In 1938 it finally recommended to council a special new committee charged specifically 'to consider ways and means of unifying the views of the Evangelical School of Thought in connection with the proposed revision of the Prayer Book,' and then apparently stopped meeting. 'A great deal depends on us,' agreed McElheran. There seem to be no further records of this group. It no doubt felt thwarted when McElheran was disabled a few months later, and ultimately evangelical opponents of prayer book revision were disarmed by the appointment of Ramsay Armitage as secretary of the General Synod committee on the matter.

At the end of January 1939 McElheran was struck with a coronary thrombosis, possibly a result of stress, overwork, and worry. In the next months, periods of apparent recovery alternated with periods under an oxygen tent. During the summer, Dean Coggan visited often and comforted the family, sometimes spending the night if an emergency seemed imminent. Ultimately, McElheran asked his friends to cease praying for his recovery. His end in this world came on 12 August 1939. He recited the hymn 'Rock of Ages,' listened to Coggan's prayers, asked after his son, and recalled his love for the people of Winnipeg. 'I have finished my course,' he said near the end, 'but tell the young men to go forward!' Canon Cody officiated at his funeral in St Paul's; two thousand attended. His body was buried in St James' Cemetery.

McElheran's ideals and Wycliffe's were nearly indistinguishable during the 1930s, partly because McElheran was personally committed to a school of thought shared by many of his associates, partly because he constitutionally enjoyed considerable authority in the college, and partly because, too diligent to be willing to delegate many of his powers, he left his own impress in so many areas. He loved the college, not merely as one loves a community, which is no stronger than its members, but as one loves an ideal or a symbol, which transcends its worldly realization. He may have failed in his dream of a national religious revival, but he spoke to thousands of people by his purity of heart, his singleness of purpose, and his deep faith.

By another public, it is true, McElheran and his college were identified, negatively, merely by what they disapproved. They stood visibly against Anglo-Catholicism, against Communism, against certain liturgical practices, against dancing and drinking and playing cards on Sunday, against, some thought, colourful academic hoods.

But, who can say whether the college could have survived as well without McElheran at the helm? He prevented the college from drifting aimlessly. He preserved the college's network of popular support. He offered certitude in a period of turmoil. He practically personified the traditions of the institution. And perhaps in proclaiming the ideals of loyalty he helped Anglicanism survive; it is remarkable that of those who graduated from Wycliffe in the 1930s, about ninety-five per cent entered the 1950s in the service of the church. Who is to say that McElheran was not just as necessary in the household of faith as the temporal householder who, as winter gales approach, bolts the doors and secures the storm windows and protects his home from ruin?

War and Peace

The Principalship of Ramsay Armitage
1940-1959

ROBERT FINCH

World War II was in its second year when Major the Reverend Ramsay Armitage, M.C., D.D., became the fourth principal of Wycliffe College. He was the son of one of Wycliffe's most representative graduates, Archdeacon W.J. Armitage, preacher, scholar, and author. Born in St Catharines, which he affectionately calls 'the garden city not only of Ontario but of Canada,' he evinced in childhood his love of gardens and a propensity for cultivating them in both a literal and a metaphorical sense. In Halifax, where his father was rector of the oldest Anglican church in the Dominion, St Paul's, founded 1750, young Armitage began, as a boy, amid the monuments of what has been called 'the Westminster Abbey of Canada,' the development of that sense of history which has so largely contributed to his effectiveness as teacher and preacher. At the same time, he strengthened a bond with the Maritime provinces which has led him to describe himself as 'a Nova Scotian, by adoption.'

After taking his B.A. degree at Dalhousie University, he went out to Western Canada College, Calgary, where he not only taught young westerners and played on their rugby team but also fell in love with the beauty of Alberta's mountains and the brilliance of its climate. Meanwhile, he had made up his mind to train for the ministry. On informing a Toronto professor, an Anglican, of his decision, he received the comment: 'Oh, you'll just love Trinity.' 'But I'm going to Wycliffe,' said Armitage. 'You couldn't,' objected the professor, 'no gentleman ever went to Wycliffe!' Cheerfully Armitage replied: 'Don't you remember what it says in the Scriptures? — And they took the poorest of the land and they made them priests unto the

Lord.' That answer, speech made with grace and seasoned with salt, was typical of the principal-to-be.

In Western Canada College, Ramsay Armitage had taught Latin. During his early student days at Wycliffe he was a tutor in Greek. In 1913, he was awarded an M.A. degree, with honours, by the University of Toronto. His choice of a thesis subject, 'The Genitive and Ablative of Quality in the Poems of Homer and Virgil,' was triply symbolic of the chooser. It not only revealed the deep interest he took in both words and poetry. Genitive and ablative are concerned with agents, manners, places and times of actions or events, and the relations of these to other persons or things. Ramsay Armitage was similarly concerned. This was soon to be illustrated in practical fashion when, as a theological student, he became prime mover in the founding of the Wycliffe College magazine, *Cap and Gown*, of which he was the first editor. Realizing that, up until then, the Alumni Association had been the sole tie for the binding together of students, faculty, and graduates, he saw the magazine as an additional means of enabling the three groups to exchange news of college, parish, and mission-field, and views on evangelical matters. At the same time, he assisted in launching less formal centres within the college for the discussion of sociological and theological topics, thus establishing a tradition still maintained. *Cap and Gown* continues to flourish and also constitutes a record of unique value.

In 1913, Ramsay Armitage was ordained deacon and appointed assistant curate at the Church of the Messiah. He was ordained priest in 1914. Then, following graduation from Wycliffe, and a short period of teaching at Upper Canada College, came a step which was the natural outcome of the effect of World War I upon many Wycliffe students, whose attention Professor Griffith Thomas, in particular, had continually drawn both to the underlying causes of the struggle and to the wider question of war in relation to Christianity: he joined the 3rd Battalion (Toronto Regiment) as chaplain. In this capacity he continuously assisted men in need with every conceivable kind of help and was indefatigable in writing to relatives of the sick and wounded. He was also constantly with the troops in the front lines and often with the forward troops under attack. In 1919 he received the Military Cross for conspicuous gallantry.

After the war Ramsay Armitage taught in Hong Kong, briefly, yet long enough to appreciate an Oriental ambience and to observe that, when one gets to know them, there is no difference between Eastern students and those of the West. He then returned to the Church of the Messiah where, reckoning from the beginning (except for the years of military duty) he served successively as curate, vicar, and rector for almost a quarter-century. During that time he not only knocked at every door of the parish but also built the parish hall. These two kinds of activity were to predominate throughout his eventual principalship, as a result of his vigilant preoccupation with the spiritual well-being of the college members and the material well-being of the college fabric.

While serving at the Messiah, Ramsay Armitage maintained close relations with Wycliffe, taking his B.D. degree there in 1925 and continuing on the staff as lecturer in Greek. He also kept up his connection with the army. Still chaplain to the militia, he was the animating spirit at weekly parade evenings and also took a keen interest in the welfare of ex-members of his own war unit, who regularly attended divine service in a body twice a year at the Messiah until 1936. In that year, when he was called to the West, each of his interwoven careers was recognized. The Church of the Messiah erected a stained-glass window in remembrance of their rector's remarkable period of unstinting care; the militia, in token of his long and effective service, awarded their chaplain the Efficiency Decoration; while Wycliffe College, in view of his appointment as dean-elect of Christ Church Cathedral, Vancouver, gave its distinguished graduate a Doctor of Divinity degree, *honoris causa*.

During his four years in British Columbia (1936-40), Ramsay Armitage entered fully into the life and work of the church, acted as senior chaplain of Military District No. 11, and at the same time absorbed the peculiar charm of the Pacific coast. He is fond of quoting:

Two Voices are there: one is of the sea,
One of the mountains, each a mighty Voice.

'That's Wordsworth,' he says; then adds, with a smile, 'That's Vancouver.' He might very well add: 'That's Ramsay Armitage,' since whatever part of Canada he stayed in, from East to West, he never failed to pinpoint its particular beauty.

Called in 1940 to be principal of Wycliffe, his coming was of a twofold nature: the return of an old friend, who had already contributed much to the college; the arrival of a new friend, who as a result of widened experience and broadened sympathies had now more to offer than ever. He was also fully aware that the college of which he was now principal, though not opposed to clerical gentility, stood for something incomparably deeper.

This, from the start, he made unmistakably plain, but with different emphases, in his three opening addresses. His address to staff and council restated Wycliffe's principles and defined the reason for the college's existence. 'Wycliffe College,' he said, 'was founded and continues primarily as a divinity school to train men for the Evangelical ministry of the Church of England. It also represents both historically and actually a great cause in Canadian life. More than any other single factor Wycliffe College has kept the Church of England in Canada Protestant and therefore free from certain practices which run counter to Prayer Book principles.' He added: 'Our task in Wycliffe College concerns the whole church. Our concern is not only with our present students but with the whole graduate body.' This conception of the inclusive function of Wycliffe, already adumbrated in the founding of the college magazine, was to characterize the nearly two decades of Dr Armitage's principalship. His address to the students appropriately emphasized the spirit of the men of the college, and ended with Bishop Pilcher's lines:

We heirs of Wycliffe's glorious name ...
Mid clouds and darkness forward go,
    Glad heralds of the Lord,
Come gain or loss, our pride the cross,
Our boast God's conquering Word.

His address to the graduate body underlined the rule which governs men from the day they enter Wycliffe College to the end of their lives: 'Our ministry, related to reality, calls for all that we can give, — it means constant, planned, continuous study, all the way.' The reference was clear: 'Study to shew thyself approved unto God, a workman that needeth not to be ashamed, rightly dividing the word of truth,' for throughout the principal's three addresses shone the motto of Wycliffe: *Verbum Domini Manet.* No words were ever more timely and it is noteworthy that Ramsay Armitage thenceforth prefaced each year of his leadership by citing the college's motto and principles.

For the duration of World War II, the principal acted as chaplain of the 2nd Battalion of the Royal Regiment of Canada and it may here be recorded that veterans of both wars regularly keep up attendance at his present church in Maple, where they have installed a plaque to commemorate the gatherings with their padre over so long a time.

The years of World War II were not easy ones for Wycliffe College nor for its principal. During World War I, (to paraphrase the eminent war-historian, Michael Howard), images, such as the Slough of Despond, Christian's Burden, the Valley of the Shadow of Death, the Good Shepherd, had been part of the collective subconscious of what was still in the main a Christian society. The childhood of Canadian students who grew up in the inter-war years had been marked by reverent purchases on November poppy days, two-minute silences at the base of soldiers' monuments on campuses, or hushed remarks about relatives killed overseas. But with World War II all this began giving way to a new generation's expression of horror and contempt for a world they claimed their parents had made. Wycliffe students were fully alive to the situation. The age for national service having been extended, military drills made heavy demands on their time, while enlistment in the ranks reduced their numbers from year to year, as both graduates and undergraduates accepted the challenge. Not the 1914-18 challenge of a 'starry-eyed vision in which the horrors were seen through a golden mist,' but, as the students put it, 'the challenge of a Reign of Terror,' 'the challenge of a world gone mad,' to which they added the challenge of Archbishop Temple: 'We are fighting to preserve the world of democracy, in which we may exercise religious freedom.' In that final challenge they recognized the unchanging fact to which war gives renewed vividness, the fact which Professor Griffith Thomas, though in other language, had pointed out to their predecessors during World War I. Thus, when in 1940 the CBC offered a fine war series called *Let's Face the Facts*, the students of Wycliffe were already quick to observe that 'the great battle of the ages being a spiritual battle, the one fact overlooked was the fact of sin.'

The call to arms, as given on the one hand by the principal in his addresses and on the other by the circumstances of war, was answered at once in a variety of ways. The Wycliffe Missionary Society which had lapsed in 1933 was revived. Wycliffe began a *Let's Face the Facts of Evangelism* through broadcasts and pamphlets for the forces. Students undertook chaplain services along the Alaska Military Highway or set forth 'The Padre's Hour,' a new basic training in religion for men of the army. All these activities having to do, in one way or another, with the presentation of the Word, attention was drawn to the necessity for making such presentation still more effective. With this aim, the college launched a department of practical theology, concerned with the spoken ministry of students in churches, Sunday schools, missions, and projects of all kinds. Here, in addition to regular training, students received lessons in voice production and public speaking under the direction of the well-known specialist J. Campbell McInnes. Moreover, as an extension of such work, the principal and members of staff visited different parts of Canada, aiding and encouraging student ministers who, throughout the war years, because of the shortage of men, were in great demand to carry on the work of evangelism both during term, in Toronto, and during the summer months, in the Maritimes, Quebec, Ontario, the Western provinces, the Peace River district, and along the British Columbia coast. The appointment of a capable and devoted travelling field secretary, Canon J.W. McDonald (Canon 'Mac'), enabled the college to keep in close contact with such effort and to promote its intelligent expansion. The war might limit the company of the evangelists, it spurred the improvement of their efficiency.

A further stimulus to the improving of that efficiency was now provided by a new project, that of ameliorating what lay at the heart of Wycliffe activities — preaching. The leader in the project was Professor Coggan, and his series of three lectures, under the title of *The Preacher as Biblical Student*, may be said to have grown straight out of the principal's opening addresses, since, as the sole means of spiritual revitalization, they presented 'God's conquering Word.' While granting that war always raises theological problems in a terribly acute form, the lectures emphasized that, in times of both war and peace, the presentation of such problems depends most particularly on the preacher who, as Dr Coggan quotes from Wesley, is 'a man sent from God to persuade men to put Jesus Christ at the centre of their relationships.' Such a man's preaching, Dr Coggan declared, must be threefold. First, because of the Person Who is its subject, the preaching is bound to be prophetic; second, it must have the positive note of one who knows the coming Lord of Whom he speaks; and, third, the speaker must be so well acquainted with the Bible as to be able to show that 'the New Testament lies hidden in the Old and the Old is made clear in the New.' The lectures, fresh and pertinent today as when first delivered, furnish a precise example of what is meant by practising what one preaches, all three of them being prophetic, positive, and Biblical.

The repercussion of these lectures on the life of the college was immediate and telling. It was decided to inaugurate a school of preaching to be held during the spring of 1941 and, in order to augment facilities for wider Biblical research, it was further proposed that the Wycliffe library be renovated and made available for use by graduates outside the college.

Canon H.J. Cody, president of the University of Toronto, on addressing the newly installed principal had said: 'You are fortunate in the staff you inherit. In my judgment there is no finer theological group in Canada.' This group, in addition to their regular tasks and their extra duties in replacing men who, because of the war were away from their parish churches, now undertook the preparation and realization of the school of preaching, while one of their number, Professor W.E. Taylor, became the moving spirit in the closely related job of enlarging and revising the library.

The 1941 School of Preaching, made financially possible through the generosity of Colonel Leonard, and with Professor Coggan as dean, offered a strenuous all-embracing programme. Mornings were spent in lectures concerning questions of matter and manner. Afternoons were taken up with the preaching and criticism of sermons delivered by students and the analysis of their voices as registered on records by CFRB and on mirror-phone by the McLennan Laboratories. This intensive work, the first of its kind in Commonwealth theological colleges, not only received special comment in English church papers, as likely to be adopted in the old country, but at once spread from Wycliffe to other colleges, with schools of preaching being held subsequently in Saskatchewan, Alberta, the Peace River District, and British Columbia. At home, students benefited by hearing at first-hand about the preaching experiences of their elders, as when Professor W.E. Taylor, on receiving a Doctor of Divinity degree, *honoris causa*, gave them recollections of his own student ministry in the early days or as when Canon McDonald shared with them his reflections of a modern field secretary. Throughout these activities it was steadily remembered that 'Schools of Preaching will accomplish nothing, but if the Spirit of God will design to work through them we shall see a return to that threefold emphasis which Charles Simeon makes in his *Horae Homilecticae* — To humble the sinner, to exalt the Saviour, to promote holiness.'

Professor Coggan's lectures, in 1940, on *The Preacher as Biblical Student*, had led naturally to the 1941 School of Preaching, in which such a student could learn how to apply his Biblical studies with 'proper assurance, earnestness and openness of style.' In 1942, there followed most appropriately what may be called a school of living, a series of lectures by members of the teaching staff in which the student was forcefully apprised of the life a preacher or, for that matter, a Christian, must lead. The theme was the Evangel, the Good News, Jesus Christ Himself, and the life portrayed gives the series its title, *Continuing Steadfastly*, since the lectures examine the five chief aspects of what it means to 'continue steadfastly in the Apostles' teaching and fellowship, in the breaking of bread and the prayers.' The lectures also warn that no school of living is alive except the transforming power of the Evangel be at work 'revealing and realizing new discovery of God and closer fellowship with Jesus Christ.'

That same year, 1942, brought home the close connection between Wycliffe College and the Bible in yet other ways. The great medieval historian, Professor G.G. Coulton of Cambridge, then living in Toronto, delivered in Wycliffe a series of ten lectures on *The Historical Prelude to the Reformation*, lectures which received a striking complement. During the six preceding years, five memorial windows had been installed in the chapel, depicting epoch-making events in English Biblical history and at the same time adding an aesthetic distinction to the chapel's appearance. These windows and their significance were now described by Professor F.D. Coggan in *The Story of the English Bible*, a short but richly informative volume, dealing with the subject both in general and in particular. Thus, to the School of Preaching and the School of Living, the windows themselves and their verbal interpretation added a School of Scripture. To these three schools, each in its own way dealing with the expression of God's gifts to man, was next added, in the same fruitful year, a School of Prayer, dealing with the expression of man's reply to the giver of all gifts. This school, summed up in *Our Response to God*, a brief and pithy book by Professor F.W. Dillistone, presents prayer as 'the essential corollary to Revelation,' pointing out that 'prayer is not man's work or discovery or achievement but God's work in man' — 'for we know not what we should pray for as we ought: but the Spirit Himself maketh intercession for us with groanings that cannot be uttered.'

One may venture to state that as a result of Dr Armitage's strong reaffirmation of Wycliffe's principles in wartime came the strong reconfirmation by staff and students of how those principles operate, in the realms of preaching, living, Bible study, and prayer. Nor in the latter realm were the many absentees forgotten, as is shown in the petition made by Hal Pink, then a Wycliffe student:

Lord Jesus, Chief of every Christian soldier, Whose life was given, Whose blood was shed for us, strengthen our brothers now on active service and let them feel Thy presence in the ranks. There at the heart of every duty, from dawn's first bugle to the last Lights Out and through heroic hazard in the night, be Thou their Guide. Keep them from evil. Lift them if they should stumble. When days are dark, grant them to see Thy light. And may they win for Thee and us the victory that shall enshrine Thy truth, Thy power, Thy love. We ask it in Thy glorious Name. Amen.

Our Response to God closes with yet another invocation in time of war, the prayer of Francis Drake bound for Cadiz where lay ships intended for the Armada to invade England:

O Lord God, when Thou givest to Thy servants to endeavour any great matter, grant us also to know that it is not the beginning but the continuing of the same until it be thoroughly finished which yieldeth the true glory, through Him that through the finishing of Thy work laid down His life, Jesus Christ our Lord. Amen.

In the spirit of this prayer, life was carried on in Wycliffe College during the war years and the years that followed, the 'great matter' in question being to put into active use the fourfold lessons of the schools. The doing of this began of course with each individual member of the college in the privacy of his own room, and from thence spread to groups spontaneously formed by the students themselves. But since, as the principal put it: 'There is always in a Theological College the danger and tendency of taking spiritual values for granted,' morning and evening services were held every day, at regular hours, in the chapel, thus providing an orderly means for constant fellowship in worship, scripture, praise, and prayer.

While Wycliffe College never asked that its students be exempted from military service, activities, both within and without the college walls in so far as possible, were carried on as usual. Yet even the business of communal living was given a fresh dimension. With the extension of the age for national service, Wycliffe, as a federated college of the University of Toronto, where so many other residences had had to be taken over for war purposes, felt it should do something to lighten the burden by admitting men of different professions and points of view. Students representing the arts, architecture, education, engineering, law, medicine, and the social sciences, poured in. They were at once made to feel at home in the Wycliffe family and not only offered a valued contribution to local discussion in general but brought a novel stimulus to the literary, debating, and athletic societies of the college and, in some cases, to its theological groups. The practice of appointing a senior medical student as house doctor was begun and many recall how much more than merely a good insurance investment this proved to be, especially in the case of 'Mac' Eagleson, now a leading Ontario physician. It is on record that the newcomers were gratified with their accommodation and, although rationing and shortages occasioned difficulties in the serving of meals, the four successive matrons of 1940-59, Miss Pidgeon, Miss Short, Miss Jarvis, and Mrs Duff, showed uncanny ability to deal with this long-drawn-out emergency situation and maintained a standard of home-cooking that satisfied even the most capacious of student appetites.

Not only were students able to enjoy the cheerful atmosphere of refectory and matron's living-room, they were also made welcome at the principal's home. From the very first, Dr and Mrs Armitage won all hearts, and visits to their home became a highlight of college life. Once a week some thirty to forty members of the college were asked in to meet staff and other guests at an afternoon tea whose delicious home-made sandwiches and cookies were prepared by Mrs Armitage herself. During the winter months, students were often entertained around the Armitages' comfortable living-room fire, singing, chatting, and enjoying the refreshments that invariably followed. A number of outside university staff members and students, who had formed a chamber music group but had nowhere to practise, were offered periodic use of the Armitages' piano. One evening, a member of the group, a young European student, whom the war had dispossessed of everything but wit and courage, announced that, after impatiently waiting the required five years, he had that very day become a Canadian. At the end of the practice, Mrs Armitage appeared, bearing a freshly baked cake with one candle, in celebration of a new Canadian's first day. For that citizen, now a scholar of worldwide reputation, the light of any candle still recalls the kindness of his hostess. Similar thoughtful gestures, equally unlooked for and equally appropriate, heightened the many occasions throughout the year when the Armitages invited individual students and their wives or fiancees to dinner.[1] Any theolog who was married in the college chapel in summer will not forget the reception that followed, given

---

1 Marriage, such a vexed question in the '30's, became a fact of college as well as extramural life during and after the war without any fuss or fanfare.

in honour of the bride and groom by the principal and his wife, in their garden. This was a place of beauty, the result of Mrs Armitage's greenest of thumbs and the principal's plentiful supply of green elbow-grease. At the same time that these two incredibly kind souls enabled so many members of the college to enjoy a second home, they also gave shelter in the upper regions of their spacious house to a series of people who had no home at all and who ranged all the way from a wartime refugee, through young couples just starting out in married life, to a struggling scholar with no place to write his *magnum opus* in peace. Nor did those who came to beg at front and back door go away empty-handed. (Since the principal's house was on Queen's Park, such visitation was an almost daily sight.) As for the birds, they had no need to beg, with two well-filled feeding stations always at their disposal, to the pleasure of students whose desks overlooked the Armitages' garden.

Two outstanding events occurred in 1943. One was the holding of the second school of preaching. This was carried on with the same ardour as before, again under the leadership of Professor Coggan who, this time, in speaking of *The Preacher's Task*, reminded the students that 'Of all the actions of the Christian ministry, preaching is the highest, and the test of our reverence for our profession is our performing of the preacher's duty.' The other event was not unrelated to this statement. In 1931, the College of Heralds had established the Wycliffe coat of arms on which appears the motto 'Verbum Domini Manet.' In February 1943, the Wycliffe hood was at last definitely determined. It stands for those arms and is worn by those who preach in accordance with that motto. The new hood was first introduced into widespread use on Easter Day of that same year, when with one exception all members of the staff occupied pulpits outside the city. Moreover, staff and students wore it both near and far that summer, in local and rural communities, among them the Indian and Eskimo residential schools in the north, a work given special encouragement and support by Bishop White who had done so much for the Canadian church in China and by the Reverend Professor George M. Wrong, who had so brilliantly occupied the Chair of History in the University of Toronto, both graduates of Toronto and Wycliffe.

So successful had been the two Wycliffe schools of preaching that it was decided henceforth to hold one annually. The wide imitation of this example and the increasing benefits derived therefrom were gratifying outgrowths of Wycliffe's initial undertaking, above all the consequent linking of college with college across the Dominion which resulted in a collective and Canada-wide raising of the standard of preaching. The prayers of the Friends of Wycliffe (founded in 1943 by Canon McDonald) were being answered. Meanwhile, no fewer than fifteen graduates were serving in the armed forces and forty-five graduates as military chaplains.

The following year, 1944, the principal's report faced the hard fact that the continuance of the war was having 'a marked effect upon all the Church of England Theological Colleges across Canada.' Enrolments had been going down steadily until 'the low water mark touched in the First Great War had almost been reached.' There were also other hard facts to face. After a stay of seven years at Wycliffe, both Professors Coggan and Dillistone were called back to England. These situations were dealt with in true Wycliffe style. The more its students in divinity were reduced in number, the more the college redoubled its efforts to serve the university by admitting further students from other faculties. The approaching departures of Professors Coggan and Dillistone were viewed in the light, not of what the college was losing, but of what, under God's grace, the college had gained by their stay: their contributions to the academic life and work of the Canadian church; their leadership in the establishing of schools of preaching and prayer; their visitations to graduates in parishes and missions; their tireless furthering of evangelism. There were also their writings, some of which have already been referred to. Now, just before leaving, Professor Coggan published a work which was used as the 1944 Canadian Lenten Book, *The People's Heritage*, i.e., the heritage of the English Bible. The same year additional distinction was brought to the college through the publication by the Westminster Press of Professor Dillistone's book: *The Significance of the Cross*. As a token of the esteem in which both these men and their work were held, and of Wycliffe's desire to perpetuate such happy associations, each was awarded the degree of Doctor of Divinity, *honoris causa*. The same honour was also conferred on Professor Horan, on his completion of twenty-five years of able service, during which the Irish charm, wit, and candid convictions that adorned his conversations and lectures won him the respect and affection of undergraduates, graduates, clergy, and laity alike.

Such degrees, bestowed on men from the old country, may be said to reflect the principal's announcement, in 1944, that he wished to work against any programme of isolationism and would like to strengthen relations between the church in England and in Canada. Wycliffe College was from the outset knit to the old land. It took its very name from John Wycliffe, one-time master of Balliol, who was exhumed and burnt, his ashes being cast into the Brook Swift, because he 'unlocked the Bible to the common English reader.' 'Thus,' wrote Thomas Fuller in 1655, 'the ashes of Wycliffe are the emblem of his doctrine which is now dispersed all the world over.'

In 1946, the principal visited England. Part of his account of this journey explains perhaps better than anything else his special feeling for Wycliffe's historic heritage. He writes:

There are particular choices which every visitor to England will make in accord with his particular interests. In my case: the Roman stronghold at Richborough; Sussex Downs; Ebbsfleet where the first 'Englishman' set foot in England and the missionary Augustine at a later date; Stonehenge; Lutterworth where John Wycliffe ministered and where runs the Brook Swift; Herne where Nicolas Ridley was vicar and where under his leading the Te Deum was first sung in English in Public worship, symbol of the Reformation in our Church of England, whereby, in the freedom of the spirit rather than in an excessive multitude of ceremonies, men might worship God from the heart and with the understanding; Bedford where the *Pilgrim's Progress* was written; Olney where John Newton and William Cowper wrote the *Olney Hymns*; St Martin-in-the-Fields (where Dr Armitage's great-grandfather once was minister); and last but far from least 'a wood outside Cambridge to hear the nightingale sing.'

Then, characteristically, he goes on to say: 'More important than visiting places was the opportunity of meeting many of our evangelical leaders in the Old Land and 24 out of our 35 Wycliffe graduates serving in England.' The principal saw to it that the links ran both ways. On the same occasion he engaged the Rev. R.F. Hettlinger of Cambridge to be professor of systematic theology at Wycliffe. Similarly, he encouraged Wycliffe graduates, such as Geoffrey Parke-Taylor and William Coleman, to round out their theological studies in England before joining the Wycliffe staff. Even yet more characteristically, on his return to Canada from England, the principal continued his visitation of graduates, from Fort William to Winnipeg, crossing the prairies by the northern route, returning by the southern, and taking in the Pacific coast and the Japanese communities around Slocan. He, and Mrs Armitage who accompanied him, herself a life-member of the Dominion-wide Women's

Auxiliary, were thus able to see many graduates and their wives in charge of remote parishes, especially in the dioceses of Keewatin, Brandon, Saskatchewan, Saskatoon, and Kootenay.

Such a well-balanced appreciation of the virtues of the Old Land and the New was typical of Principal Armitage with his strong feeling for history. During his principalship he was untiring in his efforts to keep that balance true, not only in himself but in the college. Yet circumstances were inevitably changing and when, during the summer of 1950, the principal again went to England and also to Ireland to seek people suitable for appointment to the staff, he found that, as a result of the war, men were in short supply. Moreover, members of the Wycliffe College Council now declared themselves against Old Country appointments and in favour of making their policy increasingly Canadian. The principal, ever alive to the necessity for change, yet unwilling that it entail the loss of tested worth, accepted this growing point of view with certain reservations, his conviction being 'that the universities of Great Britain and Ireland produce a type of scholar other than our own and that there is richness in diversity.' This attitude was again more than justified when subsequently from overseas the Reverend Gerald Gregson, Canon T.W. Isherwood, Canon Bryan Green, and Bishop Stephen Neill came out as missioners, and Professors H.F. Woodhouse and Ronald Ward as staff members. However, by 1957, the principal, while still pointing out 'the value and importance of keeping our links strong and direct with the Old Land,' himself made the admission: 'We have come to a time in our Canadian life when we do not need to turn so often to our nurturing mother but we are grateful all the same.' Ever increasingly did the principal, and with him the college, place emphasis on the deep roots of the Anglican church in the historic life of this Dominion. As the principal strikingly put it: 'More than one half of our bishops must write not an English word but an Indian word when they pen their episcopal signature: Quebec, Algoma, Ottawa, Moosonee, Ontario, Toronto, Niagara, Huron, Keewatin, Saskatoon, Saskatchewan, Athabasca, Kootenay, Cariboo, Yukon.'

This gradual swing to a clear realization of the full autonomy of the Canadian church in general and of Wycliffe College in particular is strikingly symbolized by the chapel windows. During the opening years of Dr Armitage's principalship, the east windows of the chapel had successively brought into vivid commemoration the history of the Bible in England: (1) John Wycliffe, (2) William Tyndale, (3) Miles Coverdale, (4) the Authorized Version, and, (5) Modern

Versions, from Bede's time to that of the Indians of Upper Canada. During the remainder of Dr Armitage's principalship, the west windows, taking over where the east windows leave off, successively brought into equally vivid commemoration the history of the church in Canada: (1) in the East, (2) in the Mid-West, and, (3) in the North, the Arctic, and the Far West.

Paradoxically the chapel windows may also be said to symbolize the unbroken relationship between the church of the Old Land and that of the New, as witnessed by the Lambeth conferences, which recurrently link the two together so effectually that, as Principal Armitage put it: 'Each Lambeth Conference is a fresh step forward in the life and progress of our Canadian Church.' Had not the Lambeth Conference of 1948 substantiated Wycliffe's claim that 'man's disorders and conflicts are primarily due to ignorance or rejection of the true understanding of his nature and destiny as revealed by God in Jesus Christ?' Were not the very subjects of the Lambeth of 1958, which the principal attended the year before he retired, the same to which Wycliffe had always given first consideration? — (1) The Holy Bible, its authority and message, (2) Church History and the Church Universal, (3) Progress in the Anglican Communion, (4) The Reconciling of Conflicts between and within Nations, (5) The Family in Modern Society. If the raising of the standard of preaching may be called a landmark in the Wycliffe of 1940-59, the double significance of the chapel windows may be called another.

While the war's end naturally brought Canada and England in some ways closer together than ever before, it left them, along with everything else, completely altered. The capitulation of Germany, the sudden surrender of Japan, had ushered in the atomic age with a train of new local and international problems. Yet above and beyond, still loomed the greatest problem of the centuries, that spiritual battle which a Wycliffe graduate, Canon (now Bishop) F.H. Wilkinson, in an address broadcast from St Paul's Church, Toronto, at the end of the war, called *The Conquest of Unbelief*. 'Looking back,' he said, 'we clearly see that the evil forces which attacked our nations not only knew that we of the Christian democracies were unprepared to defend ourselves, but that also we were spiritually as well as physically disarmed.' He went straight to the heart of the matter: 'History without Christ is purposeless, as men without Christ are powerless.' The mere sharing of material things, he declared, though part of God's command, is not enough. 'We must also share our faith in God, in His good purpose and in His primary law that, first loving Him, we should love our neighbour as ourself.' As one of the students summed it up: 'We have a duty of Hope in this darkness.'

In other words, while the world had changed, the task of Wycliffe had not. But in one respect the atmosphere of the college was drastically altered. Men were returning by the thousands to Canada, a question on their lips: 'How are we going to get back into civil life?' Many chose to do so by way of the universities and enrolment in theological colleges went up again, though with a difference. Most of the new students were older men who, because they had voluntarily foregone the natural privileges of youth, had been thrown against the raw material of life in barracks and battle. Their determination to make up for lost time induced a gratifying spirit of combined emulation and competition. The disparate age-groups which now assembled in class-room, refectory, study, or common-room, bent on the same goal, enjoyed a profitable exchange of widely varying points of view, all the more so because suddenly Indian, Chinese, Negro, and Canadian found themselves meeting together. The Literary Society, previously distinguished by such able poets as Cristobel Bendall and Maurice Walsh, was now marked by an equally sincere but more prosaic, not to say aggressive, tone. Athletic teams could once again choose from more bodies and even bigger brawn for the increasingly frequent inter-college matches. Fire drill, neglected during war-time, was resumed under the strict direction of an ex-commando whose orders were promptly obeyed, especially when the said commando was Norman Ballard, D.S.O., who could carry two recalcitrant students upstairs, one under each arm, or who, on being attacked, along with classmates, in Queen's Park by a group of thugs, laid them out singlehanded. Practical jokes came into force, as when freshmen were treated to a sophomoric tubbing, or when the tradition was established of welcoming a man back after his first experience of the newly reinstated formal dances, to find the entire contents of his room, in regular position but transferred to the ground floor so as to face him inside the front entrance. At least one of those so served went to bed then and there, a comfortable solution he was not long left to enjoy.

Such outbursts of high spirits only threw into deeper relief the students' main concern: their 'duty of Hope in this darkness,' a subject they discussed from every angle with an eagerness that sprang from a feeling of urgency. The post-war mission of the church, they concluded, was 'to preach Christ compellingly, but with a fresh awareness that neither individual salvation nor social righteousness is a sufficient end in itself, each being essentially a part of the other.'

Their conclusion reflected one major effect of the war — the renewed emphasis laid upon the relationship between an individual and the society he lives in. Wycliffe students considered fairly and squarely the many Christless solutions then being proposed, including the much publicized anti-Christian programme of Canada's deputy minister of health, Brock Chisholm. They examined the relationship of theology and the social sciences, the need to widen ministerial education, the question of church union, the burning post-war problem of temperance or abstinence, and the matter of women and Holy Orders which had been similarly brought to the fore after World War I.

When, in 1946, these and cognate topics were co-ordinated under the heading 'Man's Disorder and God's Design' at the first conference of the North American Interseminary Movement in Oxford, Ohio, Principal Armitage and ten students attended and in 1947 presented a full report of their findings. As a result, student attention in the college now became focused on a further series of current post-war subjects such as government, totalitarianism, nationalism, secularism, and racial discrimination. Particular aspects of such relationships were also looked into, that of minister, church, and world, that of denomination with denomination, and of parish with parish, whether urban or rural.

Coming closer to home, there was the relationship with the neighbour across the street to be considered. From the outset of his principalship Dr Armitage had been on excellent terms with Provost Cosgrave, and on the latter's resignation, in 1944, the provost-elect, Dr Seeley, spoke at the Wycliffe convocation. When, in 1945, Provost Seeley, who was to remain a bachelor for the next ten years, took over the direction of Trinity, he called on Mrs Armitage to stand in at Trinity social affairs. The result of this friendly arrangement, much to the delight of both provost and principal, was that visitors to Trinity on those occasions addressed Mrs Armitage as Mrs Seeley. From 1946 on, Trinity and Wycliffe co-operated each year in setting up their annual programmes, principal, provost, and other members of both staffs assisting, for example, in the preaching sessions of either college. In 1949, the association Witmashop (Wycliffe-Trinity-Married-Students'-Housing-Project) was formed for the facilitating of mutual service in the solving of this increasingly serious problem and, in the same year, Provost Seeley's book, *The Function of the University*, which stressed all kinds of mutual student-staff-administration service, was enthusiastically reviewed by John Grant Morden of Wycliffe, now principal of Huron College. In

1950, Dr (now Bishop) John Coleman urged the need for healing 'the anachronistic breach between High and Low which is symbolized by the existence of Trinity and Wycliffe,' and that same year, as though in response to such urging, Professor Derwyn Owen, of Trinity, was appointed lecturer at Wycliffe. In 1956, Professor Thomas Barnett, of Wycliffe, was appointed lecturer at Trinity. Other cross-appointments followed and by 1959, Trinity students were coming to Wycliffe for New Testament Greek while Wycliffe students were going to Trinity for Christian apologetics, an arrangement which the students themselves declared 'excellent.' Even inter-college student pranks grew to be amicably humorous exchanges, such as, for example, the newly initiated yearly practice of buying 'Miss Wycliffe' from Trinity. While prejudice dies hard in certain quarters, it is not too much to say that during Principal Armitage's régime, the two colleges, formerly often at loggerheads, came to agree on the dictum: 'in things essential unity, in things doubtful liberty, in all things charity.'

Meanwhile, from 1947 to 1950 as times became more normal, beneficial material changes took place. The front of the college was greatly enhanced by the skillfully organized voluntary care given its lawn and flower beds. A modification in the form of Queen's Park Crescent having provided the principal's house with a front garden, Dr and Mrs Armitage made their back garden with its tall trees into the college close, a secluded lawn for the use of all residents. The hitherto neglected Sheraton Memorial Hall was transformed into an attractive auditorium. The course in church music, first directed by George Chubb (now organist at the cathedral of Quebec) and then by Douglas Bodle (now organist of St Andrew's Presbyterian Church, King Street), gained in effectiveness through one more of James Nicholson's many generous gifts — the installation of a new Casavant organ, a gesture which was shortly to lead to the complete renovation and re-decoration of the chapel and the placing in it of a bronze plaque to commemorate the students and graduates who served in World War II.

At the same time the students introduced more variety into their extra-curricular activities. They began inventing ways and means of raising money both to help displaced students and to aid the United Appeal, their most picturesque effort of the latter kind being a Feather Fair, held on the back campus, at which the chief attraction was archery and the most accomplished archer — the principal! The Athletic Society now had representatives in every university sport. The Literary Society once again boasted poets of worth, notably

Charles Preston and Marshall van Ostram. For two years a dramatic society produced thought-provoking plays, such as 'The Man Who Didn't Want To Go To Heaven.' Christmas celebrations were augmented by Carol Night and by the Service of the Seven Lessons. But the most extensive of the new extra-curricular undertakings was the Thursday Afternoon College Meeting, instituted by Dean Hettlinger in 1949, which became a regular weekly feature, with tea and sandwiches for all, in the principal's residence, preceding a talk by some significant visitor, in the Common Room of the college. The instituting of the Thursday Afternoon Meeting had been prompted in part by reports brought in from all parts of Canada by student missionaries, both on the occasion of the annual Missionary Night and also in the course of special talks, such as, for example, those given by two post-graduate students, the Reverend Steven Wang (China) and the Reverend T.C. Thommen (South India), both of whom had visited Canada, travelling widely, and presented frank comments on gaps and weaknesses in the Canadian church, while stating that general conditions in Canada were as pagan as in the lands to which they themselves belonged. Was it time for Wycliffe's function to be reassessed as a place of evangelical training for clergy, as a missionary force, as a contributing factor towards reunion with other denominations, and as a bridge to society?

In the Thursday Afternoon meetings, in sessions of the Theological Society, everywhere in the college, staff and students began such a reassessment. They examined the undermining of the sense of God by such concepts as natural selection, biological determination, historical inevitability, dialectical materialism, and psychological fixation. They examined the undermining of the sense of nature by such phenomena as the dust-bowl, radio-active fall-out, pollution, the I.C.B.M. defence system, even the increases in world population. They examined the undermining of the sense of human nature through various forms of brain-washing and mass-conditioning. The conclusion reached was that man today is alienated from his own true self, from his fellows, from nature, and above all from God. What could Wycliffe offer towards a solution?

It was the old problem, old as time and new as the times. People were still people but their numbers were rapidly growing amid widely differing circumstances. Obviously the question was not how to alter Christian teaching in order to make it more palatable but how to communicate the Gospel so that it be more understandable, both by those brought up in a historic Christian position and also by those trapped within non-Christian relativist frameworks. Trained men were needed to meet modern man on his varied grounds. In 1951 the theologs themselves produced a symposium on the new meaning of a 'call to the ministry.' Yet the very next year, that of Wycliffe's seventy-fifth jubilee (1952), those same theologs noted that recruits for the ministry were getting fewer. The situation was general. As the principal put it: 'At present our theological colleges are not graduating a sufficient number of ordinands for the needs of our growing and extending Church.' Action was taken at once. A letter went out to the clergy, asking them to exhort young men to enter the ministry. At Provost Seeley's suggestion, one day in the year was set apart as Theological Education Sunday, while Bishop Luxton of Huron succeeded in having the claims of the ministry presented in high schools and collegiate institutes. Friends of Wycliffe and groups of graduates organized teams of teenagers who visited Wycliffe College for Young People's nights, during which they took part in every kind of theological college activity from services and firesides to lectures and athletic meets. These efforts, seconded notably by the Dominion-wide appeals of Canon McDonald and the Reverend Gerald Gregson, resulted in a notable increase of volunteers, which has continued ever since.

But a man so recruited must have special preparation to confront a newly diversified world, not only as preacher, teacher, administrator of the sacraments, and conductor of worship, but also as counsellor, social analyst, and executive. To that end a complete review of the theological curriculum was begun in 1950, when a board for the revision of studies was established (1) to safeguard the traditional foundation disciplines — Holy Scripture, Old and New Testament studies, systematic theology, and church history — and, at the same time, (2) to strengthen all courses in scope and standards, especially by means of pre-theological studies and specific honour requirements.

From 1950 on, Greek and Hebrew were required of all students. Pastoral theology, theoretical and experiential, was greatly enriched under the leadership of Canon William Prior (appointed dean in 1953) who initiated and conducted courses in clinical pastoralia, both at home and afield, and who, with the help of Canon Minto Swan, launched a course in penology, later adopted by the Council for Social Service of the diocese of Ontario. While the school of preaching founded by Professor Coggan went on vigorously as ever, another school of preaching, specifically for graduates, was started in 1954, with Professor M. Newby as dean. That same year, a school of rural studies, initiated by the diocese of Toronto in co-operation with Trinity and Wycliffe, proved so successful that in 1955 both colleges collaborated in a school of rural training. Meanwhile, ever since the establishment in 1947 of the Toronto Graduate School of Theological Studies by the four Protestant divinity colleges of Toronto: Emmanuel, Knox, Trinity, and Wycliffe, courses by both local and visiting professors became available, permitting the exchange and comparison of a wide range of viewpoints. Schools and projects alike made full use of audio-visual aids such as tape recorders and slide or film projectors. These renovations and innovations, introduced over a nine-year period (1950-9), in the interests of the best possible preparation of men for an effective ministry, also prompted an ever-growing concern as to the importance of academic status. It is worth noting that Principal Armitage, on the occasion of his final report to the board, when welcoming his successor, announced that Dr Hunt would, that same evening, deliver a first report on the subject of the college's accreditation.

Throughout the same nine-year period, practical application of the progressively available new knowledge and skills was being steadfastly made, in the light of 'Only as I know Him, can I Make Him truly known.' Undergraduates and graduates went out either on temporary or extended parish or missionary service, across or up and down Canada, to rural district, bushland, or Arctic wasteland. Group missions were held, as for example, the Mission of the Seventy, the Anglican Students' Evangelical Mission, or the joint mission conducted by students from Wycliffe, Trinity, the Anglican Women's Training College, the Church Army, and the Koinonia Fellowship. For overseas service, from 1952 to 1959, eight men went from Wycliffe, three to India, two to Japan, and three to Africa. Space does not permit mentioning these men by name but, whether at home or abroad, it must not be forgotten that they ventured forth backed by the understanding, help, and encouragement of a host of older men with whom they had been privileged to enjoy fellowship. To list only a few in addition to those already named, Canon Alfred Davis, and such men as Norman Green, T.W. Isherwood, M. Kaminsky, Marwood Patterson, and Dr Ronald Ward come to mind.

Meanwhile, as well as supporting the new developments that were taking place and caring for the college's members and its fabric, Dr Armitage had long since added to his duties as principal, teacher, and administrator that of serving as secretary of the Prayer Book Revision Committee. Demands for such revision had been made as early as 1939; the work was authorized by General Synod in 1943 and, after sixteen years of work and study, the first reading of the new Prayer Book was approved in 1959, the last year of Dr Armitage's principalship, though not of his secretaryship, the duties of which he carried on indefatigably until the second and final reading of the new Prayer Book in 1962.

It was singularly appropriate in several ways that the principal should fulfil such an important task: (1) because of his own superb qualifications as a scholar; (2) because he thus followed his father, Archdeacon Armitage of Halifax, who was secretary of the Committee of General Synod which produced the revised Prayer Book of 1918; (3) because Wycliffe College's purpose is so clearly expressed in the Prayer Book: 'To send forth men called to be messengers, watchmen and stewards of the Lord, to teach and to premonish, to feed and provide for the Lord's family, to seek for Christ's sheep that are dispersed abroad and for His children who are in the midst of this naughty world, that they may be saved through Christ forever.'

Characteristically, the principal gave credit to everyone but himself for the work accomplished: having cited in particular the names of Bishops Carrington, Clark, and Hallam, and those of Doctors Harrington, Millman, Naughton, Prior, Soward, Swanson, Wilkinson, and Ward, he then thanked the whole church for help in the sending out of enquiries and the gathering in of answers from all over Canada. There could perhaps be no better opportunity than the present for giving credit to the chief co-ordinator of the whole proceedings, to him who on one occasion memorably declared: 'A devout Frenchman said *The New Testament is Jesus Christ written down.* And I say *The Prayer Book is the Church of England written down.*' That was in 1955. The same year, when 'Church of England in Canada' was changed to 'Anglican Church of Canada,' Ramsay Armitage was one of the two who voted against the change. Yet to him more than to any other one man, the Anglican Church of Canada owes its new Prayer Book.

The Anglican Church of Canada and its colleges were eager to show their gratitude. From coast to coast Ramsay Armitage was honoured in many ways, and in particular by being given, in addition to the degree of Doctor of Divinity, *honoris causa*, already held from Wycliffe, similar degrees from the University of King's College, Halifax, Nova Scotia; Trinity College, Toronto; Huron College, London; St John's College, Winnipeg; Emmanuel College, Saskatoon; the Anglican Theological College of British Columbia, Vancouver. He also received the degree of Doctor of Laws, *honoris causa*, from McMaster University, Hamilton. So many honours sat well on one who had judiciously bestowed so many honours on others, though never, he tells us, had he done so with more heartfelt satisfaction than in the case of Canon 'Mac' and Canon William James, both graduates of Wycliffe. The former is known to all who love Wycliffe and the latter should be. A world-renowned authoress who met Canon James in his early days as a missionary at Baker Lake later ridiculed him in one of her books because he did not play cards. Canon James stuck it out at Baker Lake for twenty-eight years, in service to God and his flock, though his hands had to undergo a series of painful operations in order that he might handle the dog-teams. Those who saw those hands receive his degree will never forget them.

On the occasion of making his final report, Dr Armitage first gave thanks to God, then expressed his joy at having been principal for nineteen years, with three such chairmen of the Board of Trustees as the Hon. Mr Justice Davis of the Supreme Court of Canada, James Nicholson, and Dr Dunlop, three such honorary treasurers as Major Errol Hethrington, Alex Dawson, and G.A. Ellis, and three such registrar-bursars as Herbert Mortimer, Harry Burch, and A.A. Atkinson. His faithful secretaries were not forgotten: Elizabeth Pringle, Irene Chittock, Norma Mortimer, 'shining lights,' and Marion Taylor, 'a shining light for the whole nineteen years.' The senior students were remembered for the support they gave him, James O'Neil, Maurice Wilkinson, and their peers. And so on, including the hall porters and the domestic staff. 'A gallant company' was the phrase in which were summed up all these associates, who recognized in their leader the most gallant of their number.

On taking leave of Wycliffe as principal, Dr Armitage remarked that it was the closing and the opening of a chapter. As usual with one so sensitive and exact in his use of words, this was no meaningless ·convention. He, more than anyone else, had helped those nineteen years of Wycliffe College history unfold, and again and again in the course of his principalship had defined that unfolding, perhaps nowhere more clearly and succinctly than when he said: 'there is a wholeness in Christian experience which may not be defined in terms of any one period of the Church's history. So we are not content nor able to rest alone in the Evangelical Revival of the eighteenth century, nor even in the Great Reformation of the sixteenth century. But,' he added, 'there are yet great values in these two points of Anglican History ... we can never be unaware of our great heritage and of our inheritance yet to win.'

There is Ramsay Armitage's principalship in a nutshell — a constant making aware at one and the same time of a great heritage and of an inheritance yet to win.

The Principalship of Leslie Hunt
1959-1975

ROLAND HARRISON

The year in which Leslie Hunt became the fifth principal of Wycliffe College was one that contained ominous, if embryonic, portents for the future. The post-war expansion of church life in and around Toronto had witnessed the establishment of a great many new parishes in the diocese, some of them on very precarious foundations of finance and church population. Now the impetus was slowing down perceptibly, and the first indications of what was subsequently to become a serious inflationary spiral were beginning to appear on the economic scene in terms of an increase in the price of land and housing. In 1959, a projection of theological student enrolment for the following decade was made and this indicated a serious downturn in both the numbers and the quality of persons applying to colleges for theological training with a view to ordination.

The social disenchantment in the United States at that country's involvement in various overseas military enterprises was still to take definitive shape, but during the late nineteen-sixties it burst out and disrupted American society in a manner unprecedented in living memory, especially as a result of the involvement of United States personnel in Vietnam. In the intellectual, moral, and spiritual realms, traditional values were being subjected increasingly to a scrutiny which would cause many to discard the ideals under which they had been reared, and to substitute instead a flimsy relativism which in the end would prove to be a far worse master. Most serious of all, personal freedom was to be questioned in the name of freedom, and some Marxist-inspired attacks upon people and property were to be marked among other things by the destruction of university and community property.

What came subsequently to be known as a 'counter-culture' was soon to emerge on the social scene and exert a compelling influence over the younger elements of the population of North America and some other parts of the world. Coming to flower also was the 'hippie' movement, in which large numbers of youthful vagrants who claimed to be seeking their own methods of 'putting it all together' chose to involve themselves in activities which for them were a means of repudiating what they scorned as 'middle class values.' Their resultant life-style was generally one of self-indulgence, spawned under conditions of filth and degradation and accompanied by the use of mind-disorienting chemicals which they quite wrongly described as 'drugs.' It was soon to be the age of the peace protesters and of the 'flower children,' whose catchword was 'love,' a concept which for at least some of them was expressed in terms of genuine community.

That same decade was to witness the open espousal of sexual perversions, and a widespread repudiation of Judeo-Christian moral values which hacked viciously at the integrity of the marriage relationship and the solidarity of the family as the principal unit of a stable society. While well-known evangelists were continuing to proclaim the Christian Gospel with great energy and conviction in their attempts to persuade men and women to commit their lives to Christ, theologically liberal bishops in the Anglican church were combining forces with like-minded theologians elsewhere to proclaim to all and sundry the news that 'God is dead.' Towards the end of the decade these same theologians would be solemnly adjuring the clergy to dispense with their Bibles and substitute Harvey Cox's book *The Secular City*, or worse still, Richard Bach's *Jonathan Livingston Seagull*, in an attempt to be 'relevant' to the modern situation and avoid offending people by employing such forms of religious witness as mentioning the name of God in conversation.

Much of this revolutionary thinking was mercifully hidden in the future as the nineteen sixties dawned and Leslie Hunt took over from Ramsay Armitage. The Anglican church of Canada was still basking in the expansionist aura of the nineteen-fifties, and to that extent was quite unprepared for the tensions and struggles which were to wrack her and usher in a period of uncertainty and decline. The new principal had grown up and been educated in Toronto, graduating from the University of Toronto in 1930 with a B.A. degree, and from Wycliffe College in 1934 with the Licentiate in Theology. During his academic career he acquitted himself with great credit, and like others of his contemporaries he was equally proficient on the playing field and in the classroom. A man of great energy, spiritual dedication, and evangelical zeal, he was ordained in 1934, and commenced a parish ministry which was to be undertaken entirely within the city of Toronto. From a very early period in his life Leslie Hunt had been influenced by a desire to become principal of Wycliffe College, and in order to equip himself properly for this position he embarked upon a course of post-ordination study which culminated in the award of the General Synod Bachelor of Divinity degree in 1937. Subsequently, he qualified for the degree of Master of Theology in 1954, awarded under the auspices of the Toronto Graduate School of Theological Studies. Pursuing further work in the area of New Testament studies, Leslie Hunt registered for the General Synod Doctor of Divinity degree by examination, and in 1959 was successful in obtaining this qualification. The award was based on his thesis entitled *Principalities and Powers*, which comprised a study of cosmic spiritual influences in the New Testament and contemporary Judaism. Meanwhile, in recognition of his contribution to the ecclesiastical life of the diocese of Toronto, he was appointed a canon in 1956.

Until recent years, most Anglican theological colleges had appointed as their principals men who had previously spent their ministry in a parochial rather than an academic setting. Although Principal Hunt was considerably better equipped academically than most principals of theological colleges, he felt the need for a closer understanding of what was involved in the day-to-day administration of a college. Accordingly, he decided to remedy the situation by beginning his principalship with a series of visits to theological colleges on this continent and in Britain, in order to acquaint himself with the conditions under which they were working and the problems which they expected to encounter in the future.

His principalship was soon marked by an event of international significance. In August 1963, delegates from 340 dioceses of the Anglican communion scattered throughout the world converged in Toronto for the Anglican World Congress. During the preceding four years Dr Hunt had been acting as vice-chairman of the programme committee for this event, and the success of the congress was due in no small measure to the labours of that group.

The main emphases of the congress were made by the then archbishop of Canterbury, Dr Michael Ramsay, who declared that a church which lived to itself would die by itself, and by the then archbishop of York, Dr Donald Coggan, who read to the delegates a document entitled 'Mutual Responsibility and Interdependence in the Body of Christ.' This material had originated with the London meetings of the archbishops and the executives of the missionary societies, and was intended to arouse united action and participation throughout the Anglican church. It emphasized the potential role of the younger, less developed segments of Anglicanism in Christian witness, and urged the better-established areas to support them and encourage their development.

As part of the congress programme, Wycliffe and Trinity colleges held a joint convocation in the Convocation Hall of the University of Toronto on 19 August. Among those honoured by the conferring of degrees were the archbishops of Canterbury and Uganda, the primate of Australia, the metropolitan of India, and the presiding bishop of the Protestant Episcopal church. In a lengthy address the archbishop of Canterbury stated his great gratification on seeing, as he entered Wycliffe College, the long list of names written in gold of those who had gone out from the college to serve in the mission fields of the world. In the context of the Anglican Congress, these remarks constituted appropriate recognition of the international service which Wycliffe College had long rendered in the cause of Jesus Christ.

The Anglican Congress was hailed with enthusiasm as a time of Anglican rebirth by some of those who were already feeling the pressures which were building up in the areas of economics and morality. However, subsequent events were to demonstrate that this expectation was both premature and factually incorrect. Well-intentioned as it was, the Anglican Congress actually comprised a thinly veiled appeal for much larger contributions of money from the 'rich' nations in order to support the dioceses of the 'poorer' ones in the Anglican life-style.

The congress ended on a sad note for Dr Hunt when doctors discovered that his wife was suffering from an incurable illness. Her death in February 1964 was marked by many expressions of Christian sympathy to the bereaved.

Before the congress actually commenced, a beginning had been made on the task of renovating the college chapel. The sanctuary floor was lowered by one step, and the already existing space was enlarged to complete the form of the apse. A new communion rail was installed, and the panelling, the Lord's table, and the chairs were refinished in a shade of light limed oak. On a previous visit to England Dr Hunt had secured some timbers from John Wycliffe's thirteenth-century church in Lutterworth, Yorkshire, and the village wheelwright, who was also one of the church officials, had fashioned them into a six-foot cross. A Toronto woodcarver completed the plans by depicting the motifs of the four evangelists on the extremities, and the cross was then suspended from the arch of the apse to furnish an unusual and significant link with the great scholar and pioneer of the Reformation after whom the college is named. The Tippett Foundation generously underwrote the costs involved in renovating the chapel.

As its contribution to the 'Mutual Responsibility' theme of the Anglican Congress, the college agreed to accept for theological training certain men from the church in Uganda, in addition to others from India and Japan who came to Wycliffe under quite different auspices. Well aware of the cultural shock which these men would experience, Dr Hunt made every effort to help them in adjusting to Canadian ways of living after their arrival. Various churches showed a great deal of interest in the Uganda men, and in the end the college was compelled to restrict their speaking engagements and extra-curricular activities in and around Toronto so that their studies would not be jeopardized. Despite the problems presented by a prolonged absence from their families, the men adjusted surprisingly well, and by the time the programme had run its course in 1968, seven of them had graduated with the title of Licentiate in Theology, one of whom, Yona Okoth subsequently became a bishop.

Another offshoot of the Anglican Congress was the attempt made by Wycliffe to enter into a closer liaison with Trinity College, and to make stronger the good informal relationships which had existed between the two institutions for many years. Although Wycliffe College had been standing on Hoskin Avenue for more than thirty years before Trinity College moved across the street from its earlier location, there were many church-people who questioned the propriety of two Anglican theological colleges existing on opposite sides of the same street.

In the light of the historical situation which had prompted the origins of Wycliffe College, such questioning, stated in that manner, was both simplistic and naive. Nevertheless, some of those who had been approached from time to time about financial support for Wycliffe used the topographical issue as an excuse for avoiding financial responsibility towards the college, despite the fact that their number included beneficiaries in earlier days from the college's bursary funds.

Imbued by the spirit of co-operation which had been engendered by the Anglican Congress, the Wycliffe authorities decided to make a formal approach to Trinity College, feeling that the time was appropriate for Wycliffe to take up the challenge of a closer integration of witness and effort in the cause of the Gospel. It was confidently expected that a spirit of reciprocity would be evident in Wycliffe's sister college, and accordingly a committee on co-operation with Trinity College was established. A number of meetings took place which had as their immediate aim the establishment of specific academic areas in which a greater integration of work could take place as a preliminary to still wider degrees of co-operation. A programme was devised by which it became possible for students of both colleges to exchange courses at the level of elective subjects, and this continued for two or three years. In other respects, however, the repeated attempts by Wycliffe College to pursue closer integration with Trinity College met with failure, and in the end the quest was abandoned. Only subsequently and under quite different auspices was a degree of academic co-operation to be renewed.

Although the economic picture in Canada was already exhibiting some disconcerting features, there was marked university expansion evident in the province of Ontario, based upon certain population projections. The University of Toronto was involved in this expansion and the need for suitable building land on the campus caused the university officials to approach Wycliffe College in 1965 with the suggestion that a new college might be built on a nearby site if Wycliffe was prepared to surrender its present location. This proposal had some attractive features and, at an appropriate stage in the discussions which resulted, some feasibility plans were submitted for both sides to consider.

The negotiations were protracted, and while they were in progress a new element entered the picture. Emmanuel College, a United church institution located a short distance away, had approached Wycliffe on the matter of integrating its personnel and sharing accommodation in the proposed building. This enquiry was in itself a significant gesture towards the consolidation of denominational resources in the context of the Anglican-United church negotiations for union, which at that time were in progress (but were to collapse subsequently). Other organizations expressing an interest in occupying space in the 'new College' included the Ecumenical Institute and the headquarters staff of the Canadian Council of Churches. In the light of all the possibilities contemplated at that juncture a model of the 'new College' was constructed, and even this was modified somewhat in order to take account of certain other suggestions which were later made by the university.

Those who conducted the negotiations on behalf of Wycliffe emphasized quite properly the strategic nature of the college's present location, and made it clear that the alternative site and the buildings which the University of Toronto had promised to provide at an approximate cost of $3 million would have to comprise a proper and workable substitute for the Hoskin Avenue structure. These concerns were recognized by the university administrative and architectural representatives as legitimate, and discussions were carried on in a most amicable manner. In the meantime, however, inflationary and economic forces in Canada were making themselves increasingly felt and the federal government was compelled to restrict its capital funding for university and college construction. The University of Toronto found it more and more difficult to plan realistically for the envisaged cost of the 'new College' in the light of other commitments, and this factor, encouraged by a certain reluctance on the part of Wycliffe officials to move the college from its historic site, resulted in the negotiations being abandoned. For better or worse, the opportunity for the college to flourish in a new building receded with muffled steps down the dank corridors of history.

The nineteen-sixties gave full expression to the weaknesses inherent in the 'God is dead' theology of Bishop John Robinson, Altizer, and others, sometimes with startling effects. Caught up with the notion that people were living in a 'post-Christian' era, some clergy who were not particularly notable either for their display of faith or Christian experience began to talk nervously about 'being persecuted,' and muttered to one another about the church having 'to go underground.' That these reactions were nonsensical was made clear by the complete absence of anything in Canadian society approaching 'persecution,' and by the fact that the demand among laity was for the church to teach explicit Biblical doctrine and not to hide its presence in the world. Appeals had been made for some time to Wycliffe College by people in many walks of life in order to enlist the college's aid in proclaiming the truths of the Bible in a day of widespread theological confusion and ignorance, and the college responded to this evangelistic and teaching challenge in characteristic fashion. In the spring of 1965 plans were laid for what was to become known as the Lay School of Theology. The courses of instruction were offered in the evenings by the college's professorial staff, and covered the major areas of study in the theological curriculum in lectures which extended over a seven-week period in the Fall and Spring terms. Examinations were an optional feature of the programme, but for those students who successfully completed the examinations set for twelve courses in the lecture series, a certificate of Christian knowledge was awarded at the college's annual Spring Convocation. Great interest was shown in the programme from the very beginning, and the classes invariably outnumbered those of the daytime students. The lay school attracted a wide range of persons who were seeking more facts for their faith, and the academic and professional credentials of many who participated constituted an impressive testimony to the need of a faith that would minister not merely to the heart but also to the mind. The Lay School of Theology became a permanent part of the college's Christian witness, and in 1976 the first 'branch campus' of the school was established in Oshawa, to the accompaniment of requests for the college to send its faculty members to other centres also. A few of the men and women who took courses in the lay school enrolled subsequently as full-time theological students, and proceeded to ordination.

The economic pressures with which the decade had commenced increased significantly as the years progressed. As well as bringing the college into a deficit position each year, they presented real problems for the members of the teaching staff, who struggled to make ends meet on the low salaries which Wycliffe College was then paying.

At this stage faculty morale deteriorated considerably when it was realized that salaries could not be expected to keep pace with the steadily increasing costs. Those individuals who had been approached about accepting other positions found themselves torn between a desire to improve their financial lot and a concern for the survival of Wycliffe College as an evangelical witness in the church and the world. The faculty members who elected to remain at the college devised a compromise solution to the dilemma by augmenting their incomes on a part-time basis in a variety of ways. This procedure helped to maintain the current structure of the college faculty, although it had the unfortunate concomitant effect of making heavy inroads on the time and energies of staff members and diluting their contribution to the college. At the very end of Leslie Hunt's principalship the trustees were informed that, if they wanted the college to have full-time faculty members, they would have no option but to pay full-time salaries. It was to their credit that they grasped the wisdom inherent in the proposition, and set about at once to redress imbalances of salary.

Beginning in 1944, the four Protestant theological colleges on the University of Toronto campus had begun to engage in a co-operative programme of instruction at the level of post-graduate study. Known at the time as the Toronto Graduate School of Theological Studies, this enterprise offered courses for the Master of Theology degree, and was particularly useful in meeting the needs of those who wished to pursue advanced study on a part-time basis. In 1965 St Michael's College applied for admission to the school and was accepted shortly thereafter — a move which was to widen the scope of studies considerably.

The attempt to establish Christian unity as well as denominational co-operation constituted one of the religious phases of the mid-sixties, and in the realm of theological studies in Toronto it was expressed in terms of the desire of the various colleges to integrate their academic resources in the interests of providing a much more comprehensive plan of education than could be furnished by any one college. An official of the American Association of Theological Schools came to Toronto to make a preliminary survey of the situation and to act as a resource person in implementing a realistic programme of academic co-operation. A great many meetings took place at various levels, and by the beginning of the 1969-70 academic year seven theological colleges and faculties had combined their resources to establish the Toronto School of Theology. Dr J. Jocz and Dr R.F. Stackhouse, who at that period were respectively chairman and secretary of the Toronto Graduate School of Theological Studies, played an important part in the process by which the school became incorporated in April 1970. Apart from having a central office, the school operated in and through the member colleges. Its structure comprised a basic degree division, which made an extremely varied selection of courses available to persons studying for a first degree in theology, and an advanced degree division, which replaced the former Graduate School of Theological Studies. The school was now able to offer courses leading up to the Doctor of Theology degree, and soon became recognized as one of the leading theological 'clusters' on the North American continent. The original concept of the Toronto School of Theology was that of a service organization for the member colleges rather than an autonomous, degree-conferring body, and in the years that followed its inception this function provided for its affiliation with other Toronto institutions which operated on the basis of a related purpose and intent, such as the Toronto Institute for Pastoral Training. This latter organization maintained centres in nine hospitals and correctional institutions in and around Toronto, providing unrivalled resources for students and clergy engaged in clinical pastoral education.

The distinction between the basic and advanced degree levels of education had been explained in terms of purpose and function by the Toronto School of Theology *Bulletin* as follows:

> As a federated school, TST consists of distinct institutions with mutual aims. The degree of unity which characterizes TST differs with different levels of operation. At the Basic Degree level, the emphasis is on federation; the independent but autonomous colleges and faculties federate to provide effective means of coordinating the basic professional degree programmes of the participating colleges within common parameters, while affirming the continuing diversity desired by each participating college to equip persons for a variety of ministries in a variety of traditions. At the advanced Degree level, without losing the federated concept ... faculty members determine academic policy not as members of distinct member colleges but as members of the academic departments and councils of TST. TST in this respect is a school, though its faculty is drawn from the participating colleges and consists of persons who also teach at the Basic Degree level.

There can be no question that the formation of the Toronto School of Theology had the immediate effect of bringing all the theological colleges on the campus into much closer association, and to that extent it implemented a degree of ecumenicity previously unknown in Toronto. It has continued to act as a denominational catalyst, to the undoubted profit of all concerned, and this augurs well for the future of Christian ministry in Canada. But in at least one respect it has not lived up to the expectations of the colleges which agreed to participate in the venture. Instead of being able to save on educational and administrative costs, it has been shown that the member institutions are bearing a heavier fiscal burden as participants than they did when they were pursuing independent educational programmes. What effect this situation will have on the growth and character of the Toronto School of Theology is something that only the future can reveal.

As already noted, the middle years of Leslie Hunt's principalship coincided with a marked crisis of faith in many areas of Christendom. As a concomitant to the 'God is dead' theology, the pundits of that particular ideological eccentricity were solemnly advising their hearers to think in terms of such humanistic concepts as 'Christianity without Christ' or a 'church without God' if they wished to attract any kind of an audience. A number of clergy succumbed to these blandishments, and sensing an incompatibility between their newly acquired intellectual position and the historic doctrines of Christendom as expressed in the Creeds, left the ministry in order to work in what they deemed to be the more 'relevant' areas of secular activity. Potential candidates for holy orders, confused by the theological doubts which many clergy were projecting, and dismayed by the manner in which others were flouting civil and moral law alike, preferred to seek an avocation elsewhere.

The steep decline in applications for theological training which the 1959 projection had foreshadowed became an urgent reality, and Wycliffe felt the effects of the situation along with other colleges, some of which closed their doors. The challenge to faith was one which was not to be taken lightly, and accordingly the faculty members expended great effort in teaching and writing at this crucial period. During the time that Leslie Hunt was principal, no fewer than twenty-seven books and hundreds of articles for theological and other publications were written by various faculty members. This literary output far exceeded that of all the other Toronto School of Theology colleges combined, and was the largest of its kind of all the colleges in Canada. Dr Hunt's particular contribution was to give leadership in the field of evangelism, and this was to bear fruit in continent-wide efforts to win people for Jesus Christ.

What was for Wycliffe College a novel way of communicating the Christian Gospel to the public was undertaken by the then professor of New Testament, the Reverend Tom Harpur, in 1967. Approaching a local radio station, he managed to obtain listening time for a 'phone-in' programme which rejoiced in the name of 'Harpur's Heaven and Hell.' Each week some topic of importance for the Christian faith would be discussed, generally in the presence of a guest, and then the telephone lines would be opened to receive calls and comments from interested listeners. From modest beginnings the programme built up a wide clientele of avid listeners, whose penetrating questions indicated that this particular method of proclaiming the Gospel was meeting with a definite response in their minds. The programme was discontinued late in 1971 when Professor Harpur resigned his position on the faculty to become Religion Editor for the *Toronto Star*. In this capacity his academic abilities and innovative talents continued to minister the faith to an infinitely wider audience.

The year 1968 also witnessed the departure of the Reverend Norman Green from the administrative staff. A graduate of the college who had served in various rural parishes in Ontario, Mr Green had been appointed field secretary of the college by Dr Hunt in 1960. From his student days he had cultivated a keen interest in astronomy, and served from 1964 to 1972 as national secretary of the Royal Astronomical Society of Canada. In recognition of his outstanding abilities in this field he was invited to become assistant director of the McLaughlin Planetarium in Toronto, which had been constructed in 1968 on a site adjacent to the Royal Ontario Museum, with which the planetarium was structurally integrated. His acceptance of this position was yet another indication of the versatility and competence of the Wycliffe College faculty members. The trend towards expressing Christian ministry in areas other than those of traditional church structures was exemplified further by yet another talented faculty member, Dr R.F. Stackhouse, who was eventually to become Leslie Hunt's successor as principal. After graduating from the college in 1950 and serving in various parishes in the diocese of Toronto, he went to Yale University for post-graduate study and received his doctorate in 1962. Following this he was appointed to the faculty in 1963 as professor of the philosophy of religion and ethics.

For many years Dr Stackhouse had been involved at various levels in civic and political affairs, and his election to the Scarborough Board of Education in 1965 enabled him to participate actively in the field of public and secondary education at an important phase of its development in the province. For three and a half years Dr Stackhouse was also the first chairman of the Board of Governors of Centennial College of Applied Arts and Technology, Scarborough. Centennial was one of the 22 colleges of Applied Arts and Technology set up by the government of Ontario to deal with post-secondary education at a vocational level. Some, like Centennial, were totally new institutions; others were built on the foundation of existing technical colleges.

Meanwhile, his interest in the fortunes of the Progressive Conservative party led him to think in terms of giving leadership at the federal level, and in 1972 he was persuaded to contest the Scarborough East seat in the election of that year. Dr Stackhouse and his workers expended a great deal of time and effort in wooing the voters to his side, and finally the combined activities of candidate, manager, and canvassers yielded a rich dividend at the polls. He won over the incumbent member, who was a cabinet minister. When he went to Ottawa in 1972 Dr Stackhouse was the only Anglican priest to have sat in the House of Commons in its entire history. He represented his riding for two years, but when another federal election was called at the end of that period he decided not to seek re-election.

The era of Dr Hunt's principalship was marked by the elevation to the highest office in the Anglican church of Wycliffe College's most distinguished graduate, Archbishop Donald Coggan, who was also a personal friend of Principal Hunt. Four years after joining the faculty of Wycliffe College in 1937 as professor of New Testament, Dr Coggan received the General Synod Bachelor of Divinity degree, and on his departure for Britain in 1944 to re-open the London College of Divinity as its new principal, he was awarded the Wycliffe College Doctor of Divinity degree, *honoris causa.* After a few years in London he was consecrated Bishop of Bradford in 1956, and was subsequently appointed archbishop of York in 1961. It was in this capacity that Dr Coggan revisited the college at the time of the Anglican Congress in 1963. Wycliffe College rejoiced when Dr Coggan was appointed archbishop of Canterbury in 1973. The enthronement ceremony took place on 24 January 1974 in Canterbury Cathedral.

Dr Hunt had received an invitation from the archbishop himself and from the dean and chapter of the cathedral to be present at the ceremony. On his return he described the occasion in moving and glowing terms. It was, he reported, a history-making occasion which marked an advance in the whole movement of Christendom, and one on which a number of precedents was established. It was the first time that royalty had attended an enthronement, and also the first occasion on which it had been found necessary to institute measures of the strictest security in order to guard against an interruption of the proceedings by fanatical Irishmen. Those who arrived for the enthronement were dismayed to see the ancient mother-church and its precincts ringed with police and Alsatian dogs and were not a little perturbed at being searched before they were allowed to enter the cathedral. The enthronement marked the first occasion on which an archbishop with experience in the Canadian church had been elected to the primacy of Canterbury, and last but not least, it was the first time that the entire event, which was thoroughly Anglican in character, had involved many other religious denominations, including the Church of Rome as represented by some of its cardinals, thus giving the occasion a completely ecumenical and trans-racial aspect. The evangelical convictions of the new archbishop of Canterbury were made clear in his enthronement address when he stated that the church's love in Christ must reach out to embrace all people throughout the world.

The sentiments echoed by the archbishop have been those exemplified consistently by Wycliffe College throughout its history. Its strong missionary emphasis has carried its graduates into the distant parts of the earth to proclaim the gospel of Christ, often under conditions of adversity, danger, and great discouragement. Such names as Bishop Stringer of the Yukon, Bishop Fleming of the Arctic, Bishop Hamilton of Mid-Japan, Bishop White of Honan, Bishop Heber Wilkinson of Amritsar, and Charles Sadlier of Chile will never be forgotten in the history of missionary endeavour. Indeed, it was Wycliffe men who, in the closing decades of the nineteenth century, opened up to the Anglican church the frontiers of the Canadian North West. To the present time about 1000 graduates of Wycliffe have entered the Anglican ministry and have served or are serving the church in every diocese of Canada, including the Yukon and the Arctic, as well as in many other parts of the world such as Great Britain, the U.S.A., Europe, India, Japan, Uganda, Liberia, South Africa, the Philippines, and Jamaica. In addition to the great list of Wycliffe men serving God faithfully in their parish ministries, many graduates have attained high office in the Anglican church, thirty-four of them having been elected bishops up to the time of writing. Many of the college faculty members have been among the most distinguished clergymen of modern times, including such notable scholars as Canon H.J. Cody, who became president of the University of Toronto and subsequently chancellor, Archbishop Howard Mowll, primate of Australia, the Right Reverend C.V. Pilcher, suffragan bishop of Sydney, the Right Reverend W.T.T. Hallam, bishop of Saskatoon, the Very Reverend F.W. Dillistone, dean of Liverpool, and Archbishop Donald Coggan himself.

During his tenure of office Leslie Hunt always presented the challenge of evangelism to the students. Proclaiming Christ as Saviour and Lord to a world dying in sin had been at the heart of all his preaching, and as the civil and theological turbulence of the nineteen-sixties came increasingly into prominence, he voiced the need for a strong evangelistic effort to bring the peace of Christ into men's hearts. To foster this aim he himself became associated more and more closely with the Billy Graham evangelistic team, and addressed student bodies in the U.S. on various occasions. His first important contribution on an international scale came in 1966, when he read a paper as a Canadian delegate to the World Congress on Evangelism which met in Berlin that year.

The impact of this gathering on the participants was such that, like their counterparts from some other countries, the Canadian delegates decided to formulate plans for their own congress on evangelism, and Leslie Hunt was appointed chairman of the planning committee. The gathering was scheduled for August 1970 in the National Arts Centre, Ottawa, and was notable for its representative character, with 800 delegates from nearly every Protestant denomination and group participating.

Archbishop Donald Coggan, who was still at York, attended the congress as the theme speaker, addressing himself to the problem of how to communicate the gospel adequately in our time. The organizing of the congress was not without its problems, however, and in the end Dr Hunt was asked to assume the office of presiding chairman as a means of remedying the difficulties that had arisen. The affair proved to be a notable success, due in no small measure to the time and energy he had devoted to it.

The tremendous influence of the Berlin Congress and its North American successor at Minneapolis in 1969 on evangelicals generally was maintained by a group of men who planned what was to be a continent-wide evangelistic effort for 1973. It was known as 'Key 73,' and was widely advertised as the greatest thrust for evangelism in the history of North America. Leslie Hunt was the Canadian member of the Executive Committee of Key 73, and in consequence he had an unrivalled opportunity to observe the workings of the programme at first hand. About 130 denominations and groups responded to the call to proclaim the Gospel more positively to North Americans, and millions of people became involved in Bible study groups and religious education programmes. The contribution of Wycliffe College included the housing of six and a half tons of New Testaments in the basement and their subsequent distribution to appreciative students on the University of Toronto campus. As the year drew to a close it was apparent that Key 73 had exercised an important influence in revitalizing denominational spirituality and promoting ecumenical growth. Its greatest importance was in providing an opportunity for the claims of Jesus Christ to be presented in a consolidated manner to the entire North American continent.

The enthusiasm for conferences on evangelism showed no signs of abating, and in 1974 a vast congress on world evangelization was held in Lausanne, Switzerland. Some years earlier Dr Hunt had been invited to be a member of the convening council, which had to represent all the Protestant denominations of the Canadian church and to select the seventy-five Canadian delegates. The congress was intended to be the biggest of its kind in Christendom, with 4000 delegates and observers from the major denominations meeting at the historic Palais de Beaulieu. Since the delegates were coming from no fewer than 150 countries, it was obviously most desirable that instant translations of all speeches be heard in any one of seven official languages, and the technology which made this possible undoubtedly facilitated enormously the work of the congress.

Outstanding world figures were present to provide theological leadership, and experts in a wide variety of fields were available as resource personnel. The congress dealt with the theme of lay ministries and unity amongst the people of God in the world. It was designed to relate the Gospel to the social issues of modern times, and appealed to younger Christians for support in the cause of proclaiming Christ's kingdom. One prominent emphasis of the Lausanne Congress which has also been a perennial concern of Wycliffe College was the need for theological institutions to place the matter of gospel proclamation and evangelism at the centre of their programmes for the training of clergy.

The congress also brought the delegates to Lausanne face to face with the stark fact that after nearly 2000 years of Christian mission, a vast segment of the world's population had yet to be evangelized. The urgency of the situation was underlined by the presence of a 'population clock' in the foyer of the congress hall. On the first day of the meetings the convenors operated a switch and set in motion this 'clock,' which emitted a loud tick three times per second, day and night. Each tick represented another baby born somewhere in the world, and reminded delegates that during their ten-day stay in Switzerland some one million, seven hundred thousand new lives had come into existence.

The emphasis on evangelism which was so much a part of Dr Hunt's life and teaching was also exemplified in the activities of a fellow-graduate, the Reverend Marwood (Marney) Patterson. Graduating in 1955, Mr Patterson served for some time in the diocese of Toronto, becoming priest-in-charge of St James the Just, Downsview, in 1959. As his ministry progressed, he became aware that God was calling him to proclaim the Christian Gospel to the widest audience possible. Taking a decisive step of faith he obtained a leave of absence from his parish in 1963 and embarked on a series of evangelistic missions and campaigns in the diocese of Toronto on a part-time basis.

It was not long before he was in considerable demand as a parish missioner and evangelist, and when his commitments began to extend beyond the borders of the diocese, he took up evangelistic work on a full-time basis in 1966. He commenced a series of campaigns across Canada, including one to the Eskimos in the Arctic. At the same time he became deeply involved in the major evangelistic movements in the western world. He was a delegate to the World Congress on Evangelism in Berlin, acted as the executive secretary of the Canadian Congress on Evangelism in Ottawa, and attended other similar events as a delegate. In addition, he conducted seminars on evangelism and gave lectures to theological students, including those at his *alma mater*. Not content with a ministry to this continent, Mr Patterson took the gospel message to such distant countries as India, the Philippines, and Japan, in the time-honoured Wycliffe tradition.

The turbulence of university life during the period of Leslie Hunt's principalship was not reflected significantly in faculty changes, despite the dissatisfaction with salaries. Apart from the appointment in January 1973 of Dr Richard Longenecker to succeed the Reverend Tom Harpur as New Testament professor, there were no changes of personnel other than those occasioned by retirement. In 1973 the Reverend William Prior, dean of residence and professor of practical theology, reached this stage, and although he could have been reappointed on a sessional basis for a period up to an additional three years, in accordance with regulations governing the retirement of faculty members, he elected to vacate his position in favour of a younger man. Two years later, Dr Thomas Millman, professor of church history, also retired from the faculty, after serving for a short period on a sessional basis. Between them these two Wycliffe graduates had devoted forty years to the service of their *alma mater*, and perpetuated the traditions of dedication and scholarship which have been characteristic of the College's faculty. Their services were honoured suitably at the 1974 Spring convocation, when the college conferred on them the degree of Doctor of Divinity, *honoris causa*.

Another record of distinguished service was established by Miss Marian Taylor, who first began working at the college in 1934 and retired in 1969. She was a woman of great versatility who during her career acquired a vast body of knowledge about Wycliffe's history and traditions, and in many respects came to enshrine them within herself. The possessor of considerable linguistic ability, she took courses successively in Greek and Hebrew from the college pro-fessors, becoming particularly adept in Hebrew. After formal retirement she was retained on a part-time consultative basis, but finally left the college in December 1975.

From some points of view this kind of faculty stability was wholly admirable, and not least because it preserved a solid continuity of college tradition. In other respects, however, it was less desirable because it clearly worked against the best interests of the institution. The average age of the faculty and administration members was uncomfortably high, and the gravity of the situation became apparent when it was realized that four faculty members, of whom Leslie Hunt was one, would retire within a very few years of each other. Steps were taken to replace Dean Prior, and in 1973 the Reverend David W. Luck became the new dean of residence. A graduate of the college, Dean Luck had served in the mission field overseas as an educator for over twenty years, principally in India and East Africa. His wealth of experience added to his stature among both the theological students and the members of other faculties resident in the college, some of whom were Africans and Orientals. Many of these overseas students were not a little surprised when they first heard the dean addressing them in their native language, and this community of interest alone went far towards helping them to integrate into college life.

Much thought was being given also to the appointment of a new principal to succeed Leslie Hunt, whose resignation was due to be submitted in the Fall of 1975. The choice of a successor was narrowed immediately by the college's tradition of selecting its principal from among its own graduates. Of the names suggested, that of Dr R.F. Stackhouse, who was in Ottawa but was still teaching in the college on a part-time basis, was foremost. Accordingly the Executive Committee of the College met on 2 May 1974 and recommended unanimously the appointment of Dr Stackhouse as vice-principal, commencing on 1 September 1975, with succession to the principalship a year later.

When the Board of Trustees met to deal with this proposal, the decision was made to change the dates of the appointment so that Dr Stackhouse would assume the principalship on 1 July 1975. The appointment was offered to him, and after consulting his constituency association executive he decided not to seek nomination for the riding of Scarborough East in the 1974 general election which had just been announced, but instead to accept the Wycliffe College appointment.

Dr Hunt continued at the helm of the college until the end of June 1974, when he went on a year's sabbatical leave. This gave him the opportunity of accepting an appointment as warden of the Garden

Tomb in Jerusalem. Here he was able to carry on a ministry for which he was so admirably suited, preaching daily to thousands of pilgrims and tourists who visited this shrine where, according to General Charles Gordon, the resurrection had taken place. It also afforded him the opportunity of undertaking further research in the field of New Testament studies so that he might return to the college, once his sabbatical leave ended, as professor of New Testament. The college council gave a formal undertaking to this expectation by inviting him to continue as a member of the teaching faculty until June 1978. At the same time they unanimously elected him as principal emeritus, a title which had also been bestowed on Dr Ramsay Armitage when Leslie Hunt became principal.

In the lives of some men the late sixties are a time for taking things in a rather more leisurely manner, but not in the case of this busy doer of the Word. He set about his new assignment in Jerusalem with characteristic energy and enthusiasm, preparing himself meanwhile for a new and influential ministry with young people seeking to receive from him a knowledge and understanding of the New Testament that would enable them to become true ministers of the Word.

The Leslie Hunt years were a time of challenge for both principal and college. Had Wycliffe been under the leadership of a man with a less sure grasp of the essentials of the Christian faith, it might not have come through the testing-time of theological ferment with its strength intact. Had the college been directed by a principal with a less convinced understanding of what a Christian academic community should be, it could easily have suffered the sharp decline experienced by other institutions in this period. That Wycliffe was able to prepare for the advent of its second century of service for Christ with the confidence and power that it did was due to a very large extent to the resolute leadership of the man who was its mentor and guide through troubled times.

Into the Second Century

The Principalship of Reginald Stackhouse
1975-

ARNOLD EDINBOROUGH

A PLACE TO STAND

So now Wycliffe comes to its second century, a second century in what already is a very changed world. When the Reverend James Sheraton met his first nine students in St James Cathedral on 1 October 1877, Canada was a pioneer society. Although it was a newly united country, it was still a colony. The wars of Queen Victoria and the British Empire were the wars of Canada. The streets of Toronto were unpaved, the roads to the north, east, and west rough and arduous. Squared timber went out of the country, manufactured goods came in. There were no indigenous arts or music. Although the west was in the process of being linked to the east by the Canadian Pacific Railway (after much trouble), there was not really a Canadian nation. The prairies were undeveloped and the north was still a land of mystery. Gold, nickel, and copper had yet to be discovered in the quantities which have since made Canada so wealthy. Where there are now a score of metropolitan centres, there were then only two, Montreal and Toronto.

As Wycliffe has evolved in the past hundred years, so has Canada. First the railway, then the radio and, latterly, television, have put Canadians in touch with one another from the Atlantic to the Pacific. Through the immense efforts put forth by Canada during World War II, we are now an industrial nation with major manufacturing cities like Hamilton, Winnipeg, Edmonton, Vancouver, and Halifax. Ottawa, in 1877 a mere logging town chosen by the queen to be a sub-arctic capital, is now the centre of a federal government whose bureaucracy fills acre after acre of former pastureland with high-rise civil service offices. Toronto and Montreal are cosmopolitan metropolises.

In all of these cities, regardless of size, there are performing arts centres, art galleries, opera houses, museums, and sports stadiums. The people who provide the entertainment and the creative activity within those buildings are heavily subsidized by the federal, provincial, and municipal governments, and the great industrial companies which have built the Canadian economy are now as likely to sponsor a ballet, commission a play, or engage an orchestra as they were one hundred years ago to build a primitive hospital or subsidize a church school.

Such sophistication has been arrived at not only by an increase in communications, but by a century of free primary education, a half century of public secondary education, and a quarter century of freely accessible post-secondary education. It has been arrived at through the creative abilities of medical men like Wilder Penfield and the great William Osler; by scholars like Northrop Frye, Harold Innis, and O.D. Skelton; by creative artists like Jack Shadbolt, the Group of Seven, the Toronto School, Alfred Pellan, and those giants of the performing arts scene, Celia Franca, Herman Geiger-Torel, Ludmilla Chiriaieff, and Healey Willan.

Canada's society in the last quarter of the twentieth century is urban, not rural; sophisticated, not pioneer; open, not closed.

In that society there is also a much changed church. The United Church of England and Ireland in Canada (mellifluous yet faded title), whose members founded Wycliffe, has now become the Anglican Church of Canada. That church is no longer a political instrument, the kind of instrument once so ably wielded and manipulated by Bishop John Strachan and some of his successors. The Christian church as a whole, whether Catholic or Protestant, is no longer a political instrument. In many ways, indeed, the church is no longer even a social instrument.

When Wycliffe was founded, probably half the hospitals in Canada were staffed by nuns and supported by the Roman Catholic church. A great many of the schools were run by church authorities and were only just beginning to be taken over by publicly elected representatives. The kind of mission which would then give down-and-outs a meal, unwanted children a home, and unwed mothers a place to have their babies has since been taken over by government at one or other level — a government which does all these tasks and more. Though the church, somewhat atavistically, is still asked to bless babies at birth, young adults in marriage, and the elderly in death, the progression of the majority of Canadians from cradle to grave is now along lines laid down and paid for by public taxation rather than by private or ecclesiastical charity.

The church is not even a teaching instrument. Urban living means for many people rural weekends. The roads north from Toronto and Montreal, east from Winnipeg, and north and south from Vancouver are choked with traffic every weekend, choked with people going skiing in winter or swimming in summer. Sunday school is a thing of the past for most urban churches and the only place where many a clergyman can have any pedagogical impact on his congregation is in his weekly sermon to the faithful few who are still in town.

The church has changed in other ways too. Changed because of the events of the past twenty years. The backlash of the war and the silence of the Roman Catholic church in Europe as it saw Hitler send seven million Jews to the holocaust caused many in Europe to believe that God was dead. There were even, as has already been mentioned in this volume, some post-war priests of the church who preached a Christian atheism, whatever that might mean.

But Canada is not Europe and returning ex-servicemen in this country were not concerned morally with what they construed as the sordid results of megalomaniac politics. They were eager for the easier certainties of marriage and family life, a life lived within the safe confines of a new suburban home and the denominational church of their fathers. In the 1950s therefore there was such a building of churches in Canada as had not been seen since the days of the founding of Wycliffe. Church extension, as it was whimsically called in the diocese of Toronto, went on doing what had always been done in Canada: where few were gathered together at a cross-roads there was the church put amongst them — Anglican, Presbyterian, United, and Roman.

But the easy ways of the fathers were not so easily visited on the children. Some of the theological revisionism of Barth and Bultmann was seeping down slowly to the parish level. The single martyrdom of Bonhoeffer became as important as the mass-martyrdoms of Belsen and Auschwitz. The social questioning of old values in a new society — a questioning resulting from an amalgam of war-experiences, television, and an enormous increase in university education — began to take first a moral, then a theological turn. When Bishop Robinson published his book *Honest to God*, he found a ready audience. When Pierre Berton was commissioned in 1962 to write *The Comfortable Pew*, it sold more copies in the first year of publication than any other book had ever sold in Canada before.

When the Anglican World Congress convened in 1963, the opening speaker suggested that Marx, Einstein, and Freud, three German Jews, had done more in the preceding century for the furtherance of human ideals than the church. Such freedom in the ideas expressed and in the give and take of the sessions, gave new hope that the established churches (whether politically established or merely well established in the normal sense of the word) would do much for their brothers in other countries where there was an emerging nationalism, coupled with a voracious hunger for education, technology, and self-government.

But the newly self-governing countries often equated Christianity with colonialism, some expelling white missionaries precipitately, others waiting only until their own trainees could, with a minimum of dislocation, take over. In the vast land-masses of Africa and China it proved difficult to translate the sentiments of the congress into economic or social action. Then came the long nightmare of the war in Vietnam and the moral collapse of the United States presidency in the person of Richard Nixon. Youthful radicals, not the church, fought the battle of national morality there. In Canada, while Vietnam and Watergate happened, the Anglican church worried about the mechanics of Christian initiation, not a major concern of the New Testament, and the question of women priests. The North American church, in fact, slipped out of its energetic growth of the fifties to a luke-warm decline in the seventies.

Wycliffe, therefore, in training its second-century men and women for the priesthood is training them for a new society and a new church. The society is one in which the church is not taken for granted, and in which indeed it has no obvious role to play. The church must therefore reach out in new and innovative ways to keep that society on a solid moral base and to give its members the chance to know Jesus Christ as a personal Saviour in a world where the majority of social instruments are, like the computers which serve them, totally impersonal and entirely unconcerned about the human worth of the individual, let alone his immortal soul.

At such a juncture — such a critical juncture — the college needs very clear direction. The man chosen to give it that direction is Reginald Francis Stackhouse. Appointed at the age of 50, Principal Stackhouse had already had a varied career. His undergraduate work was taken at the University of Toronto, his theology and divinity at

Wycliffe and his Ph.D. at Yale. From 1950 to 1960 he was the rector of two Toronto parishes, and after his time at Yale he was appointed professor of theology and ethics at Wycliffe. By 1965 he had become a member of General Synod, the chairman of the Faith and Order Study Commission of the Canadian Council of Churches, and was a member of the doctrinal commission which for years sought to bring about the union of the Anglican and United churches in Canada.

A scholar, a committee man, and a pastor, there was yet another dimension to Stackhouse. Having first been appointed to the Scarborough Public Library Board, he then ran for office on the Scarborough Board of Education. To this he was handily elected at a time when education in the secondary schools was being heavily influenced by the turmoil on North American campuses. His involvement with parents, both as parents and electors, gave him the necessary impetus to run as a Progressive Conservative candidate in the federal election of 1972. He was elected and for the twenty-ninth Parliament of Canada he represented the 150,000 members of Scarborough East. Although his constituency would have liked him to run again in the general election of 1974, he declined, having already been offered the post of principal of Wycliffe College.

His political career, however, was only part of his outward thrust from his theological base. Principal Stackhouse's name had often appeared as a by-line in the *Canadian Churchman*, where he wrote a regular column for some years, in the *Toronto Telegram*, and in the *Globe and Mail*. In other words, Principal Stackhouse is a man whose undoubted scholarship is matched by his capacity to serve people as pastor and political representative, service which is expanded by his familiarity with the techniques of the mass media.

Joined with its sixth principal is a first class faculty, committed to academic excellence, but not only that. All are ministers of Christ and see the study of theology in terms of how it enables students to grow as persons in Christ so that they can effectively serve and lead the church.

Professor Roland Harrison is an outspoken and solid scholar of the Old Testament, while Professor Richard Longenecker is a worthy holder of the chair in New Testament. Between them, these two men have published twenty books, of which several are accepted as authoritative texts in their respective fields. After lecturing for several years in counselling, Dr Maurice Flint became professor of pastoral care and director of field education.

Dr Alan Hayes, a fluent writer and keen researcher in church history, and Dr Oliver O'Donovan, an erudite exponent of systematic theology have also brought strength to all sides of the college's life.

The vital work of the Leonard Library is under the skilled direction of Lorna Hassell, a professionally qualified librarian.

And to add still more to the college's life and work, two practising parish clergy come to the college each week to share their rich experiences and deep insights in essential pastoral training programmes — Canon Terrence Tarleton, lecturer in church music and public speaking, and Dr Leonard Griffith, lecturer in preaching.

The faculty is erudite, knowledgeable, worldly wise, experienced. At Wycliffe they zealously guard the high standards of their predecessors, but they can also move confidently outwards in a way that was not necessary fifty or a hundred years ago.

Recognition should also be given to members of the administration and faculty who, having ably served the college as it came to the centennial, moved on to other areas of service. One was Dr Leslie Hunt who had added an epilogue as professor of New Testament to his long association with Wycliffe, and on reaching retirement age began a new ministry as chaplain of Massey College, University of Toronto. Another was the Venerable A. Gordon Baker, who had been lecturer in worship as well as rector of Cronyn Memorial Church, London, Ontario, and archdeacon of Middlesex, who accepted appointment as principal of the College of Emmanuel and St Chad, Saskatoon, Sask. The Reverend Anthony Capon, who as director of development since 1975 had been in charge of administering the Second Century Fund Campaign and had been editor of *Insight*, the college's new publication, was named principal of Montreal Diocesan College. The Reverend David Luck, dean of students for five years, returned to pastoral work, joining the staff of St Anne's Church and St Anne's Towers, Toronto.

ROOTS FROM WHICH TO GROW

When Wycliffe was established, the following principles were affirmed in its charter:

1 / The sufficiency and supremacy of Holy Scripture as the rule of faith.

2 / Justification by the free grace of God through faith in Jesus Christ.

3 / One Holy Catholic and Apostolic Church, the company of all faithful people among whom the pure Word of God is preached and the Sacraments are duly administered.

4 / The sufficiency and perfection of Christ's sacrifice once made upon the cross and the priesthood in Christ of the whole Church, of which the ordained Ministry is representative.

5 / The historic episcopate, a primitive and effective instrument for maintaining the unity and continuity of the Church.

6 / The presence of Christ by his gift in the hearts of all who worthily and with faith receive the Holy Communion.

Those principles, despite the changing world, are still the principles on which Wycliffe will face its second century.

The motto of Wycliffe states 'Verbum Domini Manet' (the word of the Lord endures) and Wycliffe is committed to a biblically centred teaching. Such centrality of the Bible is inherent in all that went into the creation of Wycliffe and its continuance over the past century.

The reason is clear: unless the Bible is totally and thoroughly understood and unless its principles are deep in the heart and soul of a Christian, how can he judge the world around him? How can he feel that he has a bedrock on which he can stand in a changing world, especially in our modern world where the changes are happening so incredibly quickly?

Wycliffe graduates know this, but they must also bring that message to their people. Fortunately, the message will be gratefully received, for thousands upon thousands of Christians are now returning to the Bible themselves, not least because it is now so accessible. The New English Bible, *Good News for Modern Man* and such widely distributed versions of the New Testament as that by J.B. Phillips, have all, because of their clarity and directness of style, brought reading and meditation on the Bible back into many lives where the church is not nearly so regular a place of attendance as it once was. The statistics would be hard to arrive at, but it is likely that more people now read their Bibles without benefit of church going than they did formerly when it was merely read to them from the lectern once a week.

In this, of course, there has also been great help from such people as William Neill, whose one volume commentary on the Bible has been a godsend for many an enquiring layman and the *Gospel Commentaries* published by Penguin Books. This flow of paperbacks has been made freely available in churches and at low cost in church bookstores and has led to a concern with faith and doctrine, and with the popular interpretation of modern Bible scholarship, which far surpasses in its intensity some of the lay ferment out of which Wycliffe originally grew.

The reasons for this activity are complex, but the over-riding reason is probably that so eloquently expressed by the Reverend Arthur N. Thompson in his Alumni Lectures at the beginning of centennial year.

But what, we may ask, makes the Bible so important for the Christian? The answer, surely, is that it is the Spirit-inspired record of God's unfolding plan for man's salvation. But it is just here that so often we go wrong. In the recent paperback by Marshall and Hemple entitled *Children's Letters to God*, one little boy wrote: 'Dear God: I read your book and I like it. Where do you get your ideas? John P.' Now how many of us priests and ministers have come away, or allowed our people to come away, with the notion that religion is simply a collection of ideas about God in the hope that somehow this knowledge will help us to lead a better life?

There are, of course, world-founded religions which are essentially systems of ideas. Such are Buddhism and Hinduism. But you cannot treat the Bible like that. If there is one thing you can say about Scripture from Genesis to Revelation, it is that it is not a book of ideas, but a record of personal encounter. It is the record of how God encountered men and women as far distant and different as farmer Hosea and scholar Paul, of Ruth and Lydia, and how they responded to him. The unknown early Christian writer to the Hebrews put it all together when he began his letter: In many and various ways God spoke of old to our fathers by the prophets; but in these last days he has spoken to us by a Son (Heb. 1:1).

So while we may find some interesting ideas in the Bible, what makes it come alive for the prayerful and discerning reader is that through the Spirit who guides the reader as assuredly as he inspired the writer, we can see ourselves reflected in its pages.

Whether we see ourselves reflected in its pages, we do at least see people in its pages. As Canon Thompson implies, the problems we face in our daily lives are not new. Whether we face them in a high-rise office building in the middle of a metropolitan city, on a huge farm on the prairies, or in suffering in a hospital, the problems we face are those faced by the people in the Bible.

There is no answer to the problem of pain, but the Book of Job makes us think of it in creative ways. There is no easy solution to the hold that materialism can have on us, as the rich young man found when he asked Jesus what he should do. There is no easy acceptance of the suffering and death of a child by its parents, but the Bible shows us powerfully that cruelty, suffering, violence, and all the ills of man are not new. What triumphantly emerges from the Bible is that, if we are convinced that this is God's world, not ours, that Jesus Christ is the Saviour and that faith in Him is a personal commitment to a life better than this, then many of the problems are at least put into perspective.

Which leads to the second principle, again eloquently dealt with by Canon Thompson, that the Bible is deeply personal.

So may we in all our preaching and pastoral ministry recover this belief that he who matters supremely is the convicting Spirit and to pray that God the Holy Spirit will use our little efforts to convict the hearts and minds and consciences of our people, and also that He may convict the world in us, through the instrument of the Spirit, namely the Cross. 'We preach Christ crucified,' the great apostle told the Corinthians (1 Cor. 1:23), and while our wisdom can be used in the service of Christ, and our eloquence, if kept under strict control, what our people need more than anything else today is to see Christ uplifted, so that they may offer their love's obedience in response to his great love, and to find in his great self-sacrifice the key to a fulfilling life of service to others.

This personal commitment to Christ is what has been preached and taught and lived throughout the history of Wycliffe College. That commitment, that conviction must be the only basis on which Wycliffe can move into its second century. As Principal Stackhouse wrote recently,

This is the heart of the Christian life and the heart of the College as it performs its ministry of enabling persons to gain competence for the Ministry.

Is anything needed more in the church today? Wherever one turns, one hears men and women calling out for more meaning in their daily lives and one sees a growing number turning to all manner of cults and creeds to find it. One thing has become clear in our society. Affluence alone cannot give us the good life. We cannot spend our way to happiness. We need what can be found only through a personal faith in the Lord, and a college that helps the church to present that message is surely filling a desperate need.

BRANCHING OUT

How to present the message is a problem. But it is not a problem which is entirely in the hands of the faculty of Wycliffe College. As Canon Thompson again said in his Alumni Lectures in centennial year:

> While the Holy Spirit can be seen horizontally through history through the Bible, the Ministry, the sacraments and the worshiping fellowship, we ought also to be aware of the Spirit descending vertically from time to time, shaking us up, shattering all our pre-conceived ideas ... Are we sufficiently aware of that same Spirit abroad in the Church and in the world today? Or do we suffer from a spiritual credibility gap? Are we like the Samaritan woman at the well of Sychar who spoke of God as being active in the days of her forefather Jacob and, she believed, would be active again when Messiah came. But for her he was not here, not now. Here was her dilemma — and ours!

The task is to resolve the dilemma for those whose lives are not church-centred and who seek a sign.

Have we such signs? The answer is a resounding yes.

Take miracles. Research in this country and elsewhere done by very few men has led to the production of new strains of rice which have doubled the quantities capable of being produced in poorer countries where fertilizer is not easy to obtain. Is that not a miracle? Or the drilling of wells by simple drilling rigs which yet can probe to the water-table a hundred or more feet down in the central plateau of India, far beyond the scope of a villager's spade. And from the bore comes clear, disease-free cool and sparkling water. Is that not also a miracle?

The eradication of malaria and yaws; the control of mosquitoes; the advances in the treatment of leprosy — all are chemical miracles. New methods of communication can bring peoples together. Disasters can be met by worldwide organizations in hours, wherever they occur. The jet plane annihilates distance; satellites span space with their signals to get the jet planes into the air.

Such miracles must be seen as such. If manna was a visitation from heaven, is not food and medicine also from heaven though sent on earth-launched planes?

This vertical presence of the Holy Spirit must be proclaimed. Men do not invent; as the word in Latin originally meant, and still must mean for one who believes in God, they merely 'come upon' something not hitherto made manifest.

We have also had our prophets. Dietrich Bonhoeffer, whose letters came from prison and who, like the apostle Paul, another prison letter writer, was killed for them. Martin Luther King, who saw the promised land and led his people bravely and tenaciously towards it. His eyes saw the Glory of the Lord. Sister Theresa, who ministers to the poor in Calcutta because no-one else did. Brother Jean Vanier, who sought his mission among the mentally retarded to show that they were possessed of humanity, not the devil. Malcolm Muggeridge, Billy Graham, Pope John XXIII, prophets everywhere.

The Holy Spirit works amongst us.

What then must we do? What must Wycliffe College do as it stands on the brink of its second century?

First, it must be acutely aware of the society in which it now operates. That society is not church-oriented, but it is still spiritually hungry. If it were not, how would strange eastern cults develop in our western world? If it were not, how would transcendental meditation have taken over from what, when Wycliffe was founded, was called prayer? If it were not, why would there be astrological columns in all the newspapers and periodicals that are on the news-stands of this continent? People are looking for a power over and beyond themselves. To show the way to it, the modern Wycliffe graduate must use the means of modern communication.

Such a graduate has a model in the person of Professor Tom Harpur. Harpur realized that if his preaching mission were to be fulfilled, he could not remain in the new School of Theology, but must move out into the media. As a scholar and trenchant speaker, he was well loved at Wycliffe, but through his weekly page in the *Toronto Star* and as the religious editor of the largest Canadian daily newspaper, he has an immensely greater audience than he would have had either at Wycliffe or at Little Trinity Church where he served for so long.

Secondly, therefore, Wycliffe must analyse the means of communications available to it and its students. The kind of course initiated by Bishop George Snell in the last two or three years of

Wycliffe's first century and taken over in centennial year by the Reverend Leonard Griffith is merely one manifestation of how the faculty members are dealing with new communication. New communication means that young priests going out from Wycliffe must be able to talk to weekly or daily newspaper editors, must be able to hold their own with other civic leaders on cable television, on public and private radio and television stations and on the networks. They must be aware how programmes are put together and how their particular witness may be shaped to fit such programmes. They must also be aware that the televising of a church service is not in itself a means of communication since a church service concentrates, quite naturally, on the people who are at it, not on the people who are watching it. This is not to deny the usefulness of such great festival services as those held at Easter and Christmas which serve to remind those who are no longer part of the organized church what they have left behind them since their childhood. To be part of that whole network of modern communications needs more study and more expertise than the church generally now possesses. Wycliffe's evangelical faith must make it the leader in this new form of media mission.

Thirdly, the advances in scientific and medical knowledge make it necessary for the student solidly centred in his Bible and his theology to understand and try to interpret them in the light of his training. The question of birth control no longer bedevils the Protestant churches, but it is still a great stumbling block to faith in many Roman congregations. Abortion has already caused a good deal of concern even in Protestant churches and the question of when life begins and what life is, is going to become even more acute as scientists come ever closer to solving the ultimate mystery of life. Even if that solution does elude them, they will nevertheless be able to create artificially the conditions in which life normally springs into being. The new graduate of Wycliffe must be aware, not only of sperm banks and test tube babies, but also of such new devices as cloning, by which it is possible to create photocopies as it were of one human being in another. But he must also be able to think of such things theologically and morally. Scientists, especially geneticists, are looking for such guidance.

As medical science evolves, people will live longer and longer. We have yet to come to terms with how to deal with long life. The problems of the aging and aged, the problems of the terminally ill patient being kept alive by machines — the moral and ethical problems — are only capable of human solutions if we deal with them in the context of a living, concerned, omnipotent, and omnipresent God. The teaching in seminary must provide that context and provide the necessary liaison with the doctors whose consciences and professional ambitions may be at variance.

Fourthly, the kind of commitment which has been, and is still, asked of all Wycliffe graduates when they are called to the sacred ministry, will make of them as it has over the past century made countless others, missionaries. But then one asks the question: Where should a modern missionary serve? The mission to 'the lesser breeds without the law' is no longer possible when we have at last come to the conclusion that all the world is filled with brothers; that there is no such thing as a 'lesser breed.' We have even, through modern communications, learned that though they may in other countries be outside our law, that does not mean that their laws are wrong. There has been much ethnological and anthropological research which has caused a great deal of heart-searching in this matter and we have still to come to terms with the Christian mission to an unchristian people. Some sects have solved it by being entirely Bible-centred and unshakable in their somewhat simplistic faith first, but then proving their faith by building hospitals amongst the poor, particularly the poor of South America. At the same time they have also absorbed a good deal of the local folk heritage into their liturgy in ways in which the guitars in our chancels of the 1960s did not really succeed. Amongst other things, these fundamentalists have shown that a convinced Christian missionary has still a role to play in Africa, Latin America, and the Far East, providing he lets his convictions speak in actions rather than words.

In order for its graduates to be able to take such actions, Wycliffe must ask itself whether it should not try to persuade doctors, sociologists, and others to train as ministers, whether ordained or not. The provision of a sound Christian training at a professionally advanced level and ancillary to the medical or administrative skill may be one of the best approaches to modern mission.

Fifthly, there is a whole mission area within our own borders which is as yet untouched. If Wycliffe is to proclaim its Lord and Saviour, it must proclaim Him in our cities in Canada. This means that the faculty and its supporters must look at the kind of situation in which people are desperately seeking help and reassurance. Those situations exist in office buildings as well as in the residential areas. We need ministries in apartment complexes with apartments rented by the church to serve as a focus for both counselling and worship. We need regular services of worship and witness in the major auditoriums to be found in every large office building in every city and which are widely used by such secular groups as the United Community Fund, service clubs, and employees' fellowships. We need more than one distress centre in a metropolitan area and we need much more contact with those people who are now somewhat impersonally handled by the social welfare systems set in place by municipal and other governmental authorities.

Such witness and ministry will need new structures within the church and a new open-ness to those outside it. We must no longer expect people to come to church — we must take the church to them. Without obscuring the central mystery of worship, we must yet make it possible to worship under many circumstances and in many modes. We must also plan for the eventual break-up of the present parish structure.

A few years before the end of Wycliffe's first century, there were graduates who could not find appointments. There was an enormous amount of work to be done, yet the parish structure — a medieval holdover in many ways entirely unsuitable for modern life — could neither marshal the available resources nor deploy the already trained people.

In this area the graduates of Wycliffe can do much. But the laity can do much more. Wycliffe was founded, as this volume has already shown, by concerned laymen. As the principal wrote recently: 'Not only did the laity form the majority among its founders, but recognition of the Church as fundamentally the *laos* or people of God was one of its founding principles. The ministry of bishops and clergy has been understood as representing the people of God, not as standing between them and God in the intermediary role of sacerdotal priesthood.'

After the ferment of the 1960s, in which lay people had a strong voice for the first time, there is stagnation in the 1970s. The voice of synods is no longer the voice of the church. There is a growing tendency amongst some clergy to become once more sacerdotal. Relationships with Rome are actively pursued by leading Anglican theologians while the talks with the United Church of Canada have been summarily broken off. There is more talk of priestcraft in some circles than there is of proselytizing. The concentration on music for an audience rather than a choir to lead corporate worship is endemic in large city churches. And new rules for Christian initiation have been episcopally imposed as if the ceremony, not the sacred sinner, were more important.

If the Anglican communion in Canada is to be saved from the kind of rancour and divisiveness which originally produced Wycliffe a hundred years ago, Wycliffe must take a lead in strengthening the bond between clergy and laity. For the laity are the people of God and the church is only the visible congregation of faithful men and women.

The lay theological courses already offered must be widened and deepened. They must be offered by correspondence, by radio, by cassette, and by videotape. They must be co-ordinated by an administrative staff as practiced and as expert as those who now cope with ordinands. We do not need worker priests, but workers who are incidentally ministers of the word — and know what they are talking about.

It is imperative that the college maintain also a high academic and intellectual standard befitting its site at the heart of Canada's largest university and its status as a federated college of it. Conviction without content is not enough, and the substance of the church's message requires a theological reflection and scholarly analysis quite as penetrating and incisive as that found in any other area of study. That Wycliffe is ready to enter a new century committed to meeting that demand is evidenced in the college's seeking accreditation of its degree programmes by the Association of Theological Schools, the widely respected body that establishes and monitors standards in the seminaries of all major churches in Canada and the United States. An upturn of admissions in the last two years has returned Wycliffe to its place as the Anglican theological college with the largest enrolment in the country. But numbers are not enough. The calibre of students and the quality of programme offered them matter much, much more. Part of the accreditation process is a 'self-study' of all dimensions of the college's life, an analysis which is undertaken by a committee representative of faculty, alumni, students, and council. Their report and the findings of the A.T.S. accreditation committee will have a profound effect on shaping the academic and administrative future of the college.

It is essential to that future that Wycliffe be open to learning new and better ways of fulfilling its historic vocation. To be committed to the timeless truth of the gospel is not to be obscurantist, prone to fudging on the hard issues through fear of the facts. From its very beginnings Wycliffe chose a posture for itself as an academic community, electing to identify with the university, locating itself on the campus, its clerical and lay leaders taking their place in university

senate, its faculty and students making their presence felt. This has
not been easy because the size of its staff does not allow for much
surplus energy, and the number of its students puts a demand on all
concerned to do a share. But historically Wycliffe has stressed its role
as a federated college, and it must do so even more in the future.
Society is much better informed and discerning than it was a century
ago, and the college cannot fulfil its purpose if it confuses an earnest
desire to believe with a clear ability to know.

This will be all the more important in view of a history-making
development that is still in the formative stage but that can be
anticipated with hope. This will be a contractual agreement by the
University of Toronto, the Toronto School of Theology, and the
member colleges, including Wycliffe, by which degrees in theology
would be offered conjointly by the university and the college
concerned. The university would have representation on TST boards
and councils, and common commitment to agreed upon standards
for admission, graduation, and appointments would be required.
Approval in principle has been given by the Governing Council of the
University, and support from the colleges has been indicated. If such
an arrangement is finally worked out, it will mean greatly increased
provincial funding for theological education. Much more important,
it will mean still greater stress on educational excellence.

But the noblest aspirations of the intellect can fail if they are not
matched by sufficient financial resources to equip and maintain a
college with everything for a top-quality programme and the faculty
to implement it. Money has always been an important consideration
at Wycliffe. The college was born and grew to maturity chiefly
through the willingness of an impressively large company of
contributors, some affluent, most not, to provide what Wycliffe
needed. Their generosity gave Wycliffe a sizable endowment which
for many years guaranteed it independence. But one of the first
challenges to confront Dr Stackhouse at the beginning of his
principalship was the need to substantially increase this capital. The
endowment income which a generation earlier had paid about 85 per
cent of the budget, now could only cope with 35 per cent of it. For
several years deficits had been incurred, expenditures exceeding
income even though faculty and staff salaries were kept below the
level enjoyed by neighbouring theological colleges.

At first the prospects were not encouraging to those who thought in
terms of a major financial appeal. The celebration of the college's hundredth anniversary supplied the right occasion, but how to exploit that

occasion, auspicious as it was, was not clear at first to a college govern-ing body which had not made a major appeal for many years. Some spoke in terms of a target as small as $100,000, a veteran member of council expressing the fear that Wycliffe would be doing well if it raised enough to pay the expenses of the centennial celebration, and another cautioning would-be campaigners that the people connected with the college were so busy that a major drive could not be launched. But others had different ideas, and the council began thinking in 1976 in terms of at least half a million dollars.

For a campaign of that magnitude, first-class leadership was necessary and also professional help. Within a matter of months an impressive team of leaders from the business community was recruited, and a professional firm with proven success in fund-raising drives was engaged to give direction. Captain of the team was a new trustee, Thomas Bolton, president of one of Canada's leading food chains and a parishioner of St Matthew's, Islington, where Dr Stackhouse began his ministry. Tom Bolton soon had around him men ready, willing, and able to launch a nation wide appeal. In preparation for it, a consortium of experts was hired to make a detailed study of the building so that its trustees could know exactly what was needed. This study indicated that one and a half million dollars at least would be needed to equip the old building, first begun in 1891, for efficient service in a second century. Combined with the goal of providing the college with two endowed professorships and making essential improvements to the library, it was clear that two million dollars were needed. Spurred, maybe by sheer shock, the council gave its approval. With campaign literature created by volunteers from two of Canada's major advertising agencies and a leading public relations firm (Arthur Collins, Richard Clewes, and Charles Tisdall) with management committee meetings held weekly, under the direction of either Tom Bolton, or another trustee, Percy Fowle, who became vice-chairman, and with George Beck, vice-chairman of the College Council, as treasurer, what soon became known as the Second Century Fund, took off.

The Wycliffe community was divided into sectors, each with a target to reach and a committee of concerned persons committed to hitting the target. The first appeal was to the trustees, the faculty, and the staff. Then came the alumni and parishes with a Wycliffe connection. Major businesses were also solicited, as were founda-tions, and individuals thought to be concerned about the college. From coast to coast the appeal was made. The results have shown that there is still a large reservoir of goodwill for Wycliffe right across Canada and beyond. Those leading the drive are confident that by the end of the five-year campaign period the two million dollars will be in hand.

In addition to the money, the college will also have enjoyed the participation of a large number of persons who have devoted themselves enthusiastically and effectively to giving Wycliffe a new and vital energy.

That same energy was also created for the organization of the great centennial, a task undertaken by a general committee chaired by Dr Alan Williams, one of the college's trustees.

At the top of the programme was the archbishop of Canterbury who, with his wife, graciously consented to return to their old college for this great occasion and each to give major addresses. The Rt. Rev. John Taylor, bishop of Winchester, agreed to give three lectures on *The Theology of Evangelization*. It was hoped the thought and conviction these lectures would stimulate could provide a basis for a renewed commitment by Wycliffe to world mission. The lieutenant governor of Ontario kindly invited all the Wycliffe community to a vice-regal reception at her suite in the Ontario legislative buildings and the province agreed to host a luncheon for Archbishop and Mrs Coggan. A great banquet at the Royal York Hotel brought three days of festivity to a fitting close.

When an invitation went out to each graduate, no one could know for certain how many would want to assume the expense and effort of paying a visit to their *alma mater*. But faith was vindicated once more: hundreds of registrations were received, from not only every part of Canada, but from every continent. To express this world character of Wycliffe four representative graduates from different parts of the world were honoured at a centennial convocation: the Rt. Rev. Yona Okoth, Uganda; the Rev. Canon Redfern Loutit, Moose Factory; the Rev. Thomas Thommen, India; and the Rev. Lambert Willis, Dawson Creek.

The college building received a modest 'facial' for the great homecoming, all three floors being painted and new carpet being laid. The refectory tables and chairs were refinished, and some landscaping done. A beautiful crest bearing the Wycliffe coat of arms was placed over the main entrance, and an historical plaque was erected on the front lawn. This plaque, the gift of the province, was unveiled by the Hon. William Davis, premier of Ontario, and dedicated by the Most Rev. Edward Scott, primate of the Anglican

Church of Canada, in an impressive ceremony. Another plaque, commemorating the founding of the college at St James' Cathedral, was placed in the cathedral narthex.

The year 1977 was a great time to be part of the Wycliffe family, but all its sons and daughters knew in their hearts the inspiration they had received had been given them for a purpose. It was surely to strengthen them for a new century of service, the kind Wycliffe has shown it can give.

Leading up to all this rejoicing there was yet another strand being woven into the web of the future: the position of women in the Anglican church.

From the beginning of the seventies, when the issue became urgent, Wycliffe gave support to accepting the claim that women should have the right to enter the priesthood, all its faculty signing an 'open letter' of theologians to the church calling on it to support the change. For many years the college had served the ministry of women by providing theological courses to students of the Deaconess and Missionary Training House, later changed to the Anglican Women's Training College. The 'co-ed' character of Wycliffe classes through these years led to many marriages, including that of Dr and Mrs Stackhouse, who first met each other at the college. As well, some women had taken the full theological programme and graduated from Wycliffe. Mary Mills and Phyllis Locke, two of these, were in fact among the very first women to be ordained priests of the Anglican Church of Canada. The number of women students enrolled at Wycliffe grew steadily, as these changes took effect, and the residence itself became 'co-ed' in the last two years of Wycliffe's first century, quarters being provided for a small number of single women students. They quickly became integrated into the community's life, and so easy was the change, and so warm their welcome that an observer might have thought Wycliffe had always had women living there. Once again the college had shown that, unchanging as its principles and objectives were, it could always adapt in innovative, even radical ways, to changing times.

So, with one century behind it, and its achievements properly celebrated, Wycliffe looks ahead.

And what is its future? A very healthy one if it continues to be a college which will produce priests and members of a Church who know the world well, and can move easily within it; a college which can use communications expertly and can involve itself in the major issues of the day from a solidly theological viewpoint. But such a college gives all Christians assurance: assurance that our church will mature in ways as yet undreamed of, ways summed up cogently and movingly by Cardinal Suenens in a dialogue with the archbishop of Canterbury in 1970:

Whatever shows the Church as a community moving toward its final destiny, toward God who will be 'all in all', toward the glorified Christ, has a particular power of speaking to our time. We ourselves must rediscover the God of the Bible; the God of Abraham, Isaac, and Jacob; and not the God of the philosophers. We must free ourselves from those aspects of Greek philosophy that viewed the universe as a world enclosed upon itself, forever destined to be a cyclic whirlpool with no life movement toward the future. We must rediscover the personal God of the Bible. He is not the God who wishes to reveal to us first and foremost a series of theological propositions and theses, but the God of that promise which commits us to the future, the God who reveals Himself to us as a Love that is personal, spontaneous, unmerited, and irrevocable.

It is in this perspective that we can locate the Church between the 'already' of Easter and the 'not yet' of the *parousia*. In the Church, the past is always actual and the future is already present. In the Church, tradition means perpetual renewal and evolution means continuity. In the Church, there lives Christ who is 'the same yesterday, today, and forever.'

Secure in that knowledge, the Wycliffe family — faculty, graduates, students, brothers and sisters in Christ — will go forward with joy and hope, remembering always in its second century what St Peter said in Christianity's first: 'Simply reverence the Lord Christ in your hearts and always have your answer ready for people who ask you the reason for the hope that you have.'

Index

Acheson, E.C. 31
Armitage, Molly Ponton 74, 77, 81
Armitage, Ramsay 54, 65-87
Armitage, W.J. 24, 59, 86
Atkinson, A.A. 87

Ballard, Norman 80
Baker, Gordon 112
Barnett, Thomas 82
Beck, George 123
Bendall, Christobel 80
Bethune, A.N. 9, 11
Blake, Edward 17
Blake, Samuel 17, 38
Blodgett, John 33, 54
Bolton, Thomas 123
Boyd, Harriet 38
Brock, Irene 43
Brown, Miriam 26
Burch, Harry 87
Burwash, Dr 19

Campbell-McInnis, J. 70
Capon, Anthony 111
Carrrington, Philip 86
Chittock, Irene 87
Clark, Howard 86
Clewes, Richard 123

Cody, H.J. 14, 15, 24, 25, 33, 34, 35,
   42, 50, 63, 70, 101
Coggan, F.D. 52, 53, 63, 70, 71, 75,
   76, 84, 124, 90, 100, 101, 102
Coggan, Jean 124
Coleman, John 82
Coleman, William 77
Collins, Arthur 123
Cosgrave, F.H. 35, 81
Cotton, T.H. 25, 31
Coulton, G.G. 72
Cronyn, Bishop 7
Currelly, C.T. 28

Davis, Alfred 85
Davis, H.H. 87
Dawson, Alex 87
Denison, J. Shirley 35
Dillistone, F.W. 52, 53, 72, 76, 101
Draper, Chief Justice 17
Duff, Edwina 74
Dunlop, Dr 87

Ellis, G.A. 87

Fairweather, Eugene 14
Falconbridge, J.D. 31
Falconer, Robert 28

Finch, Robert viii
Fleming, A.L. 27, 31, 33, 101
Flint, Maurice 112
Fowle, Percy 123
Fuller, Thomas 77

Gander, Jabez 39
Geddes, Walter 30
Gould, Sidney 26
Green, Bryan 61, 78
Green, Norman 85, 99
Gregson, Gerald 78, 84
Griffith, Leonard 112
Gzowski, Casimir 17

Hague, Dyson 25, 33, 50, 59
Hallam, W.T.T. 25, 31, 32, 86, 101
Hamilton, Heber 101
Harpur, Tom 98, 104, 117
Harrington, James 86
Harrison, Roland viii, 112
Hayes, Alan ix, 112
Hetherington, Errol 87
Hettlinger, R.F. 77, 83
Hiltz, R.A. 31
Horan, B.W. 32, 50, 51, 56, 76
Howard, Michael 67
Hoyles, N.W. 24, 26, 27, 38
Hunt, H.R. 40
Hunt, Leslie 85, 88-106, 112
Hutton, Maurice 20

Isherwood, Thomas 33, 36, 51, 78, 85

James, William 87
Jarvis, Miss 74
Jocz, Jakob viii, 96
Jones, Mabel 54

Kaminsky, M. 85
Knox, Bishop 6

Leonard, R.W. 36, 71
Lloyd, G. Exton 26
Locke, Phyllis 125
Longenecker, Richard 104, 112

Loudon, James 21
Loutit, Redfern 124
Luck, David 105, 111
Luxton, George 84
Lynch, F.J. 27

Marsh, C.H. 37
Matheson, S.P. 31
McDonald, J.W. 70, 71, 87
McElheran, Brock 43
McElheran, Irene 43
McElheran, R.B. 40-64
McInnis, J. Campbell 70
McIntyre, E.A. 31, 33, 35
Medley, John 14
Mercer-Wilson, Richard 54
Millman, Thomas viii, 86, 104
Mills, Mary 125
Morden, John 81
Mortimer, Herbert 87
Mortimer, Norma 87
Mowll, Howard W.K. 25, 31, 32, 101
Mullins, J.D. 28

Naughton, McKenzie 86
Neill, Stephen 78
Newlry, M.T. 84
Newman, John Henry 5, 6
Nicholson, James 87

O'Donovan, Oliver 112
Okoth, Yona 92, 124
O'Meara, Frederick A. 23
O'Meara, Harriet Boyd 38
O'Meara, J.D. 38
O'Meara, Margaret D. 23
O'Meara, Marian C. 30
O'Meara, Thomas R. 23-39, 42, 44
O'Neil, James 87
Owen, Derwyn 82

Parke-Taylor, G.H. 77
Paterson, James 14
Patterson, Marwood 85, 103
Patton, James 17
Pepperdene, L.M.M. 33

Pidgeon, Alice 74
Pilcher, C. Venn 25, 31, 36, 51, 52, 68, 101
Pringle, Elizabeth 87
Prior, William 84, 86, 104, 105

Rainsford, W.S. 10, 11
Ramsay, Michael 90
Raymond, H.D. 31
Robinson, John viii
Rogers, Amy 26

Sadleir, Charles 32, 101
Sanson, Alexander 23
Seeley, R.S.K. 81, 84
Sheraton, James Paterson viii, 3, 13-22, 24, 25, 59, 107
Short, Dorothy 74
Shortt, Charles H. 39
Smith, John Taylor 34, 36
Smith, Nancy 54
Snell, George 118
Soward, Reginald 86
Stackhouse, Margaret 125
Stackhouse, Reginald ix, 96, 99, 100, 105, 107-126
Stiles, Sextus 33
Strachan, John 7, 20
Stringer, Isaac 101
Swan, Minto 84
Swanson, Cecil 86
Sweatman, Arthur 11, 12, 26
Sweeney, James 23, 27, 31

Tarleton, Terrence 112

Taylor, John V. 124
Taylor, Marion 87, 104
Taylor, W.E. 33, 36, 37, 49, 58, 70, 71
Tisdall, Charles 123
Thomas, Louy 32
Thomas, W.H. Griffith 25, 31, 69
Thommen, T.C. 83, 124
Thompson, Arthur 114, 115, 116
Tomkins, Floyd 26
Trees, J.D. 33
Trevett, A.C. 30, 37

Vance, Principal 35

Wallace, W.S. 18
Walsh, Maurice 80
Walsh, Walter 6
Wang, Stephen 83
Ward, R.A. 78, 85, 86
Ward, W.G. 6
Whitaker, George 7, 8
White, William 75, 101
Whitney, E.C. 36
Wilkinson, Frederick H. 79, 86
Wilkinson, Heber 101
Wilkinson, Maurice 87
Williams, Alan 124
Willis, Lambert 124
Wilson, Daniel 17
Wilson, R. Mercer 33
Woodhouse, H.F. 78
Wrong, George 18, 75

THE LEONARD LIBRARY
WYCLIFFE COLLEGE

Lightning Source UK Ltd.
Milton Keynes UK
UKHW010000210722
406167UK00001B/269